THE
FREEDOM
BIBLE

TED ADAMS

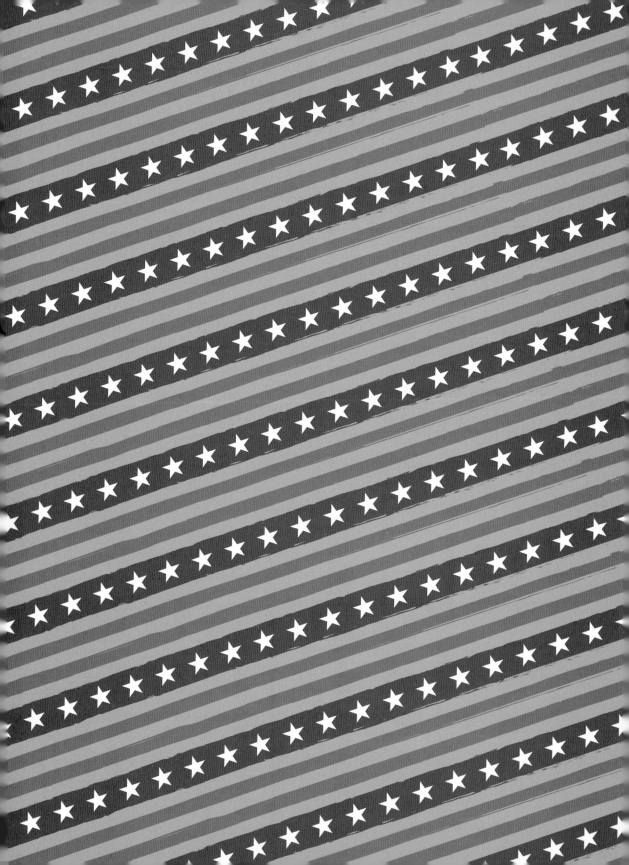

THE FREEDOM BIBLE

AN A-TO-Z GUIDE TO

★ **Exercising Your Individual Rights**

★ **Protecting Your Privacy**

★ **Liberating Yourself from Corporate and Government Overreach**

TED ADAMS

Skyhorse Publishing

All inquiries should be addressed to Skyhorse Publishing, 307 West 36th Street, 11th Floor, New York, NY 10018.

Skyhorse Publishing books may be purchased in bulk at special discounts for sales promotion, corporate gifts, fund-raising, or educational purposes. Special editions can also be created to specifications. For details, contact the Special Sales Department, Skyhorse Publishing, 307 West 36th Street, 11th Floor, New York, NY 10018 or info@skyhorsepublishing.com.

Skyhorse® and Skyhorse Publishing® are registered trademarks of Skyhorse Publishing, Inc.®, a Delaware corporation.

Visit our website at www.skyhorsepublishing.com.

10 9 8 7 6 5 4 3 2

Library of Congress Cataloging-in-Publication Data is available on file.

Design by Joanna Williams
Images used under license by Shutterstock.com

Please note: At press time, all internet addresses contained herein were valid and in working order; however, Hollan Publishing is not responsible for the content of these sites, and no warranty or representation is made by Hollan Publishing in regard to them.

Print ISBN: 978-1-5107-7478-0
Ebook ISBN: 978-1-5107-7498-8

Printed in China

"IS FREEDOM ANYTHING ELSE THAN THE RIGHT TO LIVE AS WE WISH? NOTHING ELSE."

—Epictetus

CONTENTS

Make Freedom Your Foundation

If you believe in the strength of freedom as more than an ideal, you can find smart ways to exercise it in all parts of your life!

The United States was founded on what were, at the time, radical notions of personal freedom. European settlers who made the arduous journey across the Atlantic brought with them loyalty to their home monarchs and were remotely governed by them. Succeeding generations, though, born into this vast land of promise, increasingly valued self-government and began to chafe under the thumb of distant rulers.

The result, as we know, was the Declaration of Independence and the hard-won establishment of a new country where every citizen was born with certain unalienable rights—rights that could not be taken away—including the right to freely live a life of their own choosing. It cannot be overstated how revolutionary this idea was.

We are now almost 250 years into this great experiment with freedom and democracy, and while our rights to life, liberty, and the pursuit of happiness remain, the growth of government at all levels, from community to federal, strains our ability to enjoy those rights. Advancing technology threatens not just our personal freedom but also our right to keep our thoughts, desires, and actions private. Increasing overlap and cooperation between law enforcement, government agencies, and tech companies puts nearly every aspect of our private lives under the eye of others, for their profit or for social control.

If you're concerned about this erosion of individual liberty and privacy, it's time for your own personal revolution. *The Freedom Bible* is here to help you get started. In its pages you'll learn about government and corporation intrusions large and small, and find actionable steps you can take to regain control of your own life. Don't wait another day.

Fly Freely within Your Rights

Travel these days can seem filled with screenings, rules, and sometimes roadblocks. Do you know what's truly required and how you can fly through airport checkpoints easier?

Courts in the United States have repeatedly found that the constitutional right to travel does not encompass the right to travel by any specific method. You are free to move about the country, but if you want to fly you'll have to play by the TSA and airline rules.

That said, you do still have rights as a US citizen, whether flying domestically or returning from overseas. As in all situations where you are dealing with governmental bureaucracy and its representatives (whose training, experience, and attitudes vary greatly from one person to another), your best bet is to know your rights and advocate for yourself while remaining calm and respectful. Let your emotions get the better of you and you may find yourself grounded.

What Is a Passenger Name Record (PNR)?

When you book a flight, regardless of whether you do so directly with the airline or through an online travel agent, a passenger name record, or PNR, is created. The PNR will contain your name, flight numbers, email address, and other basic info, as well as anything added later, such as seat and meal selection. If you are flying into, out of, or within the United States, your PNR will be transmitted to US Customs and Border Protection (CBP), where it will remain for up to fifteen years or until any relevant law enforcement action against you is completed. Your PNR may be shared with other governmental agencies, and you may request a copy of your PNR.

TSA Is Not Law Enforcement, but CBP Is

The Transportation Security Agency (TSA) is in charge of security of all means of transportation in the United States, but the agency is best known for its role in security screening of air travelers and their belongings.

TSA is not a law enforcement agency, and TSA agents are not police officers. They can't arrest you, but they can search you and your belongings and ask you questions about where you've been, where you're going, and the purpose of your travel. As a US citizen, you don't have to answer questions about your religious or political beliefs, and if an agent tries to pressure you into answering these kinds of questions you should ask to speak to their supervisor.

Customs and Border Protection (CBP), the agency that screens you when you enter the United States, is a law enforcement agency. While they are not allowed to profile you according to your race, religion, national origin, or other personal characteristics, CBP does not need reasonable suspicion to detain you or search you or your belongings.

DID YOU KNOW?

TSA can't arrest you, but they can search you and your belongings and ask questions.

Security and Scanning Methods

Body Scanners

Scanners currently used in the United States use millimeter wave (MMW) imaging technology that penetrates clothing but no deeper, and highlights areas of concern on a generic human outline. Those areas must then be checked by a TSA agent. MMW scanners don't use X-rays and don't reveal personal details.

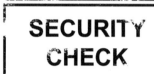

Walk-Through Metal Detectors and Wands

Metal detectors and wands use magnetic fields to detect the presence of metallic items. They utilize nonionizing radiation, which is not harmful.

Opting Out of Scanners and Metal Detectors

You have the right to opt out of body scanners and metal detectors, but if you do you will be subject to a pat-down. During a pat-down you have the right to request:

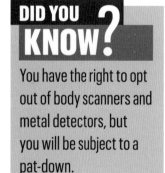

DID YOU KNOW?

You have the right to opt out of body scanners and metal detectors, but you will be subject to a pat-down.

★ The pat-down be performed by an officer of the same gender

★ A private screening, accompanied by a person of your choice

★ A chair if you need one

Opting Out for Medical Reasons

Pacemakers and implanted defibrillators are probably safe to go through metal detectors and scanners, but consult with your health care provider before flying and if there are any doubts, opt out of scanners, metal detectors, and handheld wands and request a pat-down instead. You can print out a TSA notification card and write in your medical condition or disability; this notifies TSA agents that you will require accommodation but doesn't exempt you from screening.

Swabbing for Explosives

It is considered virtually impossible to avoid getting some residue on the outside of a bag or device after you've put together an IED (improvised explosive device). The residue sticks to the hands and is transferred to the outside of the bag or container, so if you are selected for this kind of additional screening you'll have your hands and your bag or device swabbed.

Screening of Carry-On Bags

If you belong to a trusted traveler program such as TSA PreCheck, you'll be able to send your belongings through the X-ray machine without taking anything out. Otherwise, you'll have to remove your electronics, your quart-size bag of liquids, and possibly your shoes, and place them in separate plastic bins for screening.

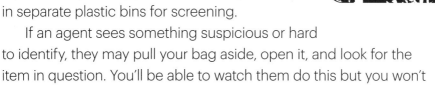

If an agent sees something suspicious or hard to identify, they may pull your bag aside, open it, and look for the item in question. You'll be able to watch them do this but you won't be able to touch your bag as they search it.

Some US airports are starting to switch from X-ray machines to CT machines for screening carry-on bags. Because CT images are more informative than X-rays, you can leave your liquids and electronics in your bag. The downside is that CT scans are much slower and can drag out the screening process.

Exceptions to Limits on Liquids

TSA regulations generally restrict the amount of liquids you can carry on to individual items of no more than 100 milliliters each, and no more items than you can fit in a one-quart zip-top bag. However, liquids (such as breastmilk, formula, juice, and liquid nutrition), gels, and pastes necessary for infant nutrition or medical conditions are exempt from limitations on quantity, as are ice packs or other means of cooling the liquids.

Screening of Checked Bags

After you check your bag at the counter, it will be screened before it is loaded onto the plane. Several screening methods are used.

- ★ **X-rays.** All checked bags are X-rayed.
- ★ **Dogs.** Canine agents are generally trained to detect drugs or explosives, although some are also trained to sniff out cash, wildlife, animal horns, or plants.
- ★ **CT scanning.** Slower than X-rays, CT scans give three-dimensional images and are usually reserved for suspicious bags. (For example, your bag might go directly to CT if you pay cash for a one-way ticket at the ticket counter.)

DID YOU KNOW?

Some canine agents are trained to sniff out cash, wildlife, animal horns, or plants.

Your checked bag may be opened and inspected; if it is, you will find a notice placed inside the bag when you pick it up. If you have a luggage lock that is labeled TSA-compliant, they will be able to open it with a master key provided by the manufacturer. Otherwise, they will cut the lock. You can lodge a complaint with TSA if you believe something has been lost or damaged during the search.

Help or Hoax?

DHS Traveler Redress Inquiry Program (TRIP)

If you are denied boarding because your name is similar to someone on the no-fly list, or if you are repeatedly selected for additional screening but don't think you should be, you can apply for redress. **If investigation finds you are not in fact on either watchlist, you'll be assigned a redress number you can add to flight bookings to avoid future problems.**

Some number of people are going to be randomly chosen for additional screening every day, though, and being chosen once in a while doesn't mean you're on a list. Having a redress number won't necessarily exempt you from ever being chosen at random.

Terrorist Watchlist

The US government Terrorist Screening Database (also known as the terrorist watchlist) is maintained by the FBI. For security reasons, you won't be told if you are on the watchlist.

There are two subsets of the watchlist:

★ **No-fly list.** If you're on it, you will not be permitted to board a plane that flies to, from, over, or within the United States.

★ **Selectee list.** If you're on this list, you will be subjected to additional screening before being allowed to board.

The Difference Between Domestic and International Travel

When you fly domestically, your rights regarding TSA's ability to detain and search you are similar to those you enjoy when you're at home. But when you are returning to the United States from another country, the airport you fly into is considered a border crossing, and the actions that can be taken by border agents are considerably more intrusive.

For example, you may be asked to unlock your electronic devices or provide your password(s) so agents may unlock them. As a citizen, you may not be denied entry into the United States if you refuse to comply, but you may be detained for lengthy screening and your devices may be seized for further investigation. To protect your privacy:

★ Travel with as few devices as possible.

★ Don't store on your device(s) emails, chats, photos, or other files you want to keep private.

★ If asked for your password, try to enter it yourself rather than disclosing it.

★ If you must give up your password, change it as soon as possible.

Programs for Expedited Security and Border Clearance

If you fly frequently, you may choose to enroll in TSA PreCheck (for domestic travel) or Global Entry (for international travel). These programs provide special lines to help you speed through security screening and border control, but they do require you to undergo significant screening beforehand. The idea is for the federal government to become well enough acquainted with you to decide you are not a threat, rewarding you with faster security clearance with no need to remove your shoes, liquids, and electronics.

TSA PreCheck

In addition to filling out an application and paying a fee, you must appear in person to be fingerprinted and have your identity and citizenship confirmed. PreCheck is available at most, but not all, US airports and with most airlines. You are not entirely exempt from additional screening with PreCheck, and it is possible that from time to time your boarding pass will not display the PreCheck logo and you will have to go through the regular security line.

Global Entry

Global Entry offers expedited entry into the United States from another country and is more expensive than TSA PreCheck. But when you sign up for Global Entry, TSA PreCheck is included with the fee. As with PreCheck, Global Entry requires an in-person interview to confirm your identity and citizenship.

NEXUS

NEXUS is an expedited entry program for entry into Canada and the United States. Currently just $50 for five years, NEXUS gives access to TSA PreCheck and Global Entry in both countries and covers land, air, and marine entry points. The only downside is that because the focus is on travel between Canada and the United States, the locations for the mandatory in-person interview are all located along the US northern border.

SENTRI

The SENTRI program allows you to use special expedited lanes when returning to the United States from Mexico by land, but not when entering Mexico from the United States. SENTRI users are also allowed to use the expedited NEXUS lanes when entering the United States from Canada.

Resources for Travel with Less Hassle

Passenger Name Record (PNR)

cbp.gov/travel/clearing-cbp/passenger-name-record

Find out what's in your PNR, who can access it, and how you can get a copy.

Security Screening–TSA

tsa.gov/travel/security-screening

Get all the details directly from TSA.

Fly Rights

transportation.gov/airconsumer/fly-rights

Read up on your rights when traveling by air, from the US Department of Transportation.

Rights at Airport Screenings and Checkpoints

elsevier.com/connect/what-are-your-rights-at-airport-screenings-and-checkpoints

See what a civil liberties lawyer and former Department of Homeland Security advisor has to say about your rights.

TSA PreCheck

tsa.gov/precheck

Learn about and apply for TSA PreCheck, the program for
expedited security screening for domestic travel.

Global Entry Information Guide

cbp.gov/sites/default/files/documents/globalentry-info-guide.pdf

Learn about and apply for Global Entry, the program for expedited
entry to the United States.

American-Made Products

Buy American!

Free yourself from overseas dependence, choose high-quality, safe products, and protect American jobs. You have the power in your everyday purchasing decisions!

There are many reasons Americans may choose to buy American-made products: doing so supports American workers and protects American jobs, keeps money from sales and business taxes in the country, and may be easier on the environment due to reduced shipping distances.

But what advantage does the "Made in the USA" label offer to you, as an individual? Why should you go out of your way to find and buy products that are American made?

Know the American Advantages

Perhaps the most obvious benefit to buying American-made products is that it reduces your dependence on goods from overseas. This has never been more of an issue than during the COVID pandemic, when supply chain disruptions led to shortages of everything from tortillas to computer chips. Suddenly the abstract became concrete, as everyday people faced empty store shelves and long delays in delivery of larger items such as cars and couches.

GOOD FOR YOU!

Buying American-made products reduces your dependence on goods from overseas.

Of course, American-made products may still rely on some components that originate in other countries, and supplies of those components may still be delayed from time to time. But overall, buying American means you're more likely to be able to get the things you need, when you need them.

Another advantage to buying American is knowing products made here are subject to stringent safety and suitability requirements. We may chafe against the burden governmental regulations place on businesses, and some companies may even move manufacturing abroad because of them. But some other countries—China, for example—have such lax safety standards that products made there may actually be dangerous for you and your family.

The Meaning of "Made in the USA"

What does it mean for a product to be American made? What's behind the "Made in the USA" label? You won't be surprised to know there's a governmental agency responsible for making that determination.

The Federal Trade Commission (FTC) was created in 1914 with the mission of protecting consumers and promoting fair business practices. One of its tasks is making sure anything labeled "Made in the USA" is, in fact, "all or virtually all" made in the United States. For the most part, American-made products don't have to be labeled as such, but the FTC will take action against a company that states or implies its products are made in the United States when they are not. You should also know:

★ **Certain categories of goods are subject to separate federal statutes that require country-of-origin labeling,** even if the country of origin is the United States. These include automobiles and textile, wool, and fur products.

★ **To earn the "Made in the USA" label, a product must be "all or essentially all" made in the United States.** This means it must be assembled in the United States, mostly with components made in the United States. Some parts may be sourced from other countries, as long as their cost and importance to the final product are negligible.

★ **Companies are free to create product labels that indicate some domestic content or processing, even if the product doesn't qualify as "Made in the USA."** For example, the label may say the product is assembled in the United States from imported parts, or that it contains a specified percentage of American-sourced components.

★ **"Made in the USA" labels don't have to be preapproved by the FTC before they are applied to goods; in most cases, it's up to each company to state their product's country of origin honestly.** (With the exception, of course, of automobiles and textile, wool, and fur products, as mentioned above.) Beware of labels and branding that tout American values and suggest an item is made in the United States without actually saying so.

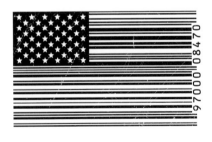

How to Tell If a Product Is Made in the USA

The best way to ensure you are getting truly American-made goods is to trust the seller, whether that's a retailer or the manufacturer itself. It's to your advantage to foster a relationship with the companies you do business with, rather than going for the cheapest goods from the biggest stores.

That said, how can you tell if a product you're interested in is made in the United States? Some level of trust in the company is still needed, but here are a few places to look for this important information.

Look on the Product Itself

US Customs and Border Protection (CBP) requires all imported products to be labeled with the country of origin. This makes determining that an item is *not* American made pretty easy. CBP regulations say the country of origin label must be on a tag or on the item itself, easily found by a casual observer, and not likely to fall off accidentally. If you can't find a country of origin label, the product is probably made in the United States. There's not much chance a company will leave you guessing about that, though—if it's American made, it will probably be proudly labeled as such.

Read the Online Retailer's Product Information

Not every online retailer will include country of origin in the information for each product, but many will. When shopping online, scroll down the product page for a section called "Product Information," "Product Details," or something similar. If the country of origin isn't stated, see if there's a section where customers can ask questions—"Where is this made?" will almost always be asked by at least one person.

Check the Company Website

Virtually every business in the United States now has a website of some kind. Check the company's site for an "About Us" tab, which should give information about when and where the company was founded, its mission and philosophy, and why it makes or sells the products it does. You can also look for a "Contact Us" tab, or look at the very bottom of the site's landing page, to see if the company and its employees are based in the United States.

Call the Company

As a last resort, you can go old school: Call the company and ask if their products are American made. This was easier to do pre-pandemic, when you had a better chance of having your call answered by a live operator of some kind. Now you may have to go

★ ★

Help or Hoax?
UPC Codes

Universal Product Codes (UPCs) were introduced in the 1970s to track grocery items but are now everywhere, on virtually everything you buy. The familiar machine-readable pattern of black and white stripes with human-readable numeric codes at the bottom provide information about a product's type, its manufacturer, and its individual identity. You may have heard that the code also carries information about the product's country of origin, making it easy for a savvy consumer to see right away where an item was made. While there's a grain of truth in this belief, **it won't help you determine whether an item is made in the United States**. To understand why, let's take a look at a typical linear, or one-dimensional, barcode.

The first digit on the left designates the kind of product, and the kind of code that will follow. Zero is a common first digit for general retail goods. Specialty goods, such as pharmaceuticals, have different initial digits. The next set of numbers indicates the product's manufacturer, and the second set identifies the individual product. The final digit off to the right is a check digit, part of a mathematical process that confirms the previous string of numbers is correct. (Credit card numbers also have check digits; that's how an online service or retailer knows you've entered a valid number.)

through several layers of option selections before reaching an actual human. If you go this route, your best bet is to try to reach someone in sales or marketing.

Resources to Help You Buy American

Businesses and websites do come and go, but at the time of publication these sites are available to help you choose American-made companies and products.

What about the country of origin? **The first two or three digits of the manufacturer's identification do indicate which country the company that bought the UPC code is based in—but that's it.** The product itself could have been made anywhere in the world, and there's nothing in the UPC code telling you that.

So if your goal is to buy from an American company—even if it imports its products from another country—the UPC code will help you with that. Country codes are set by GS1, a company that sets barcode standards and issues UPCs around the world. Per the GS1 website, codes for manufacturers based in the United States include:

00001–00009
0001–0009
001–009
030–039
060–139

For other country codes, visit the GS1 website at gs1.org/standards/id-keys/company-prefix.

All American Reviews

allamericanreviews.com

This website researches and reviews companies and their American-made products, but doesn't sell them. Reviews include information on each company's history and manufacturing practices, along with details about specific products.

How to Buy American

howtobuyamerican.com

This is the website of Roger Simmermaker, author of *How Americans Can Buy American: The Power of Consumer Patriotism*. While the book focuses on identifying American companies rather than American-made products, the website includes articles about international trade as well as links to companies that sell American-made products.

MadeInAmerica.org

madeinamerica.org

This nonprofit states its mission is to change consumer behavior through education, working with organizations such as the Chamber of Commerce to encourage Americans to buy American.

Made in America Movement

themadeinamericamovement.com

This organization works with American companies and consumers to promote American businesses. Its website provides links to companies they have vetted and approved.

Made in USA Forever

madeinusaforever.com

This California-based company sells American-made products with a stated desire to protect America's future by keeping production and jobs in the country.

Strictly USA

strictlyusa.com

This Colorado-based company sells only products it has determined are truly American made and that meet its standards of quality and usefulness.

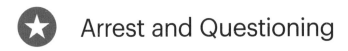

Know Your Rights in a Police Encounter

Prepare now so you don't panic or put yourself in an incriminating position! Knowing your rights in all the different types of police stops can help you navigate a law enforcement encounter with calm and confidence.

If you feel unprepared to interact with police, you're not alone. Now is a great time to put in a little reading and research to know the law and your options *before* you need them. Coming face to face with a law enforcement officer can't always be avoided, even when you are minding your own business and innocent of any crime. Although state and local laws vary, you can rely on some general guidelines and legal knowledge if you find yourself being approached by a police officer who wants to talk to you or take you into custody.

What's Permissible for You and the Police?

Having to stop what you are doing and interact with a law enforcement officer may be inconvenient at best and life-changing at worst. Your detailed rights during such an encounter depend on your state's laws, but there are some basic principles to keep in mind.

Levels of Permitted Intrusion

Each kind of law enforcement interaction has its own criteria for how long the interaction can last, what police can demand of you, and what rights you retain. A major factor in the different encounters is how intrusive the officer's behavior can be and, critically, whether they can lawfully search you and seize your property.

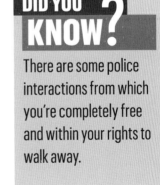

Consensual Interaction

A police officer may stop anyone in a public place and initiate conversation. They may ask questions about whether you've seen someone they're looking for, for example, or even just start a friendly chat. In this kind of situation, your consent to engage is required and you may simply walk away if you want to.

★ **How long can it last?** This is entirely up to you, as you are free to walk away.

★ **Can they search you?** No.

Community Caretaking Encounter

A community caretaking encounter is one in which a police officer has reason to believe you need help or are an immediate threat to public safety. This kind of encounter is separate from any kind of investigation into criminal activity—it is about offering assistance, not solving crime.

DID YOU KNOW?

There are some police interactions from which you're completely free and within your rights to walk away.

★ **How long can it last?** As long as it takes to make sure you are safe and receive any needed help (transport to a hospital, for example).

★ **Can they search you?** Depending on the circumstances, it might be argued that you need to be frisked for weapons as a matter of safety. The Supreme Court has ruled, though, that police performing a welfare check do not have carte blanche to search your home.

Detention/"Terry Stop"

Named for a 1968 court case, a Terry stop is one in which a police officer has reasonable suspicion that you are engaging, have engaged, or are about to engage in illegal activity. In a Terry stop you are being detained—you are not free to go—but have not been arrested. The purpose of this kind of stop is to investigate whether the officer's suspicion is valid.

★ **How long can it last?** A Terry stop must be brief. A general rule of thumb is no more than 20 minutes, but that isn't set by law. The purpose of this kind of stop is to determine whether a higher level of intrusion is called for. If it goes on for too long, it may become an arrest, even if that isn't the officer's intention.

★ **Can they search you?** During a Terry stop, an officer can, for their own safety, frisk your outer clothing (a "Terry frisk") to make sure you're not carrying a weapon. They must have a reason, based on prior experience or knowledge, to think that might be the case. However, if they find drugs or other illegal items during the frisk they can seize them as evidence (and likely progress to an arrest).

Traffic Stop

A traffic stop is, in essence, a kind of Terry stop. You are not free to avoid the encounter; refuse to produce your license, registration, or proof of insurance when they are requested; or drive away when you want to. (See page 82 for more detailed information on traffic stops.)

★ **How long can it last?** Only as long as it takes to perform the tasks involved—checking your documents, making sure you don't have an outstanding warrant, issuing a ticket, etc.

★ **Can they search you?** They can search your vehicle if they have reasonable suspicion that you are engaging in unlawful activity, for their own safety if they have reason to believe you may be armed, or if they can plainly see evidence of a crime.

Arrest

While detention requires reasonable suspicion that you may be, may have been, or may be about to engage in unlawful activity, an arrest requires probable cause—reason to believe your involvement in criminal activity is likely.

★ **How long can it last?** That's entirely open-ended.
★ **Can they search you?** Yes.

Identifying Yourself to Police

Currently, twenty-four states have "stop and identify" statutes that allow police to demand identification if they have reasonable suspicion that you are involved in illegal activity. If a police officer asks you for your identification, ask if you are being detained or if you are free to go. If they say you are free to go, you don't need to produce identification, even in stop and identify states.

> **GOOD FOR YOU!**
>
> Always ask if you are being detained or if you are free to go.

Answering Police Questions

Beyond possibly having to identify yourself, you do not have to answer any question a law enforcement officer asks you. If you are not comfortable answering questions, ask if you are being detained or if you are free to go. If you are being detained, you'll probably want to talk to a lawyer before the police. If you are not being detained, you can walk away without talking at all.

What Are Miranda Rights?

Named after a 1966 Supreme Court case, the Miranda warning ("You have the right to remain silent. . . .") is intended to remind you of your Fifth Amendment right not to incriminate yourself. If you are arrested, before they question you the police must make sure you understand you don't have to talk to them, and that you can ask to have a lawyer present before saying anything. If they don't, your answers to their questions—even if you confess to a crime and tell them everything—may not be used as evidence if you go to trial.

Understand Civil Asset Forfeiture

If you are convicted of a crime, law enforcement can seize money or other property that you obtained as a result of your criminal activity. This is called criminal asset forfeiture and it's part of the punishment.

Very different from criminal forfeiture is civil asset forfeiture. Laws vary, but generally civil asset forfeiture does not require a criminal conviction. In some cases it doesn't even require criminal charges to be filed. Law enforcement only needs to show by a preponderance of the evidence that the forfeited property was likely involved in criminal activity.

Limited Legal Rights

In an interesting variation of the usual legal process, the law enforcement entity initiating the forfeiture is the plaintiff, and the property itself is the defendant. If your property is seized by civil asset forfeiture, you are merely a claimant and typically have no right to legal representation. (One possible exception to your right to legal representation is if the property being seized is your residence.)

Once property has been forfeited, it is unlikely to ever be returned, even if you prove you were not involved in criminal activity. The claim of connection to criminality is against the property itself rather than against you, its owner. Property is usually sold at auction and the proceeds, along with any forfeited cash, may either go directly to law enforcement or to other public agencies.

The Easiest Target

Property seized by forfeiture ranges from vehicles to homes, but seizure of large amounts of cash is probably the forfeiture most likely to affect the average citizen. There are perfectly legal reasons for a person to carry a large amount of cash from one place to another, but in the eyes of law enforcement, doing so is inherently suspicious. The laws of many states make it easy to justify a seizure of cash, and hard to get it back.

Resources to Help You Know Your Rights

At the time of publication, these sites can help you stay up-to-date on your rights in interactions with law enforcement officers.

American Civil Liberties Union (ACLU)

aclu.org/know-your-rights

The ACLU provides information on what to do when facing questions from law enforcement—including police stops but also law enforcement at airports.

Help or Hoax?

Taking It to Court

In the cases of rights violations mentioned in this chapter, is it ever advised or productive to take the case to court to fight? Here's the current legal and real-life perspective.

Historically, if you incriminated yourself when you had not been advised of your Miranda rights and your statements were used inappropriately, you could sue the police. In 2022, though, **the Supreme Court ruled that the right to a Miranda warning did not include the right to seek redress** if your rights are violated when the Miranda warning is withheld.

If you face civil asset forfeiture, your only recourse is to contest it in court. Legal proceedings of this type can be lengthy, complicated, and expensive, and you risk exposing yourself to additional police scrutiny. Many who have lost money or property decide fighting forfeiture just isn't worth it. **If you do decide to contest civil asset forfeiture, get professional legal advice, and do it quickly—you'll have a limited amount of time before your property is gone forever.**

Nolo

nolo.com

Nolo has an extensive library of free legal articles—including an encyclopedia that helps define terms such as *arrest* versus *detention*. The site search makes it simple to find what you need.

Protect Your Assets and Credit

Don't give up on your dreams! You can come back from bad luck on your path to financial freedom. Here's how to successfully use the system designed for fresh starts and hold off bully creditors.

A run of misfortune—a severe injury or an illness that leaves you unable to work, for example, or an economic downturn beyond your control that destroys your business—can leave you buried under a mountain of debt you simply cannot overcome. Although bankruptcy may seem like personal failure, it is intended to help you survive financial disaster and get a fresh start. Not everyone qualifies for bankruptcy in every situation, though, and while shedding the burden of debt may be a huge relief, the negative consequences may haunt you for years to come. So it's important to do your research and consider your choices carefully before taking this path to gain financial freedom.

What Is Bankruptcy?

In its simplest terms, bankruptcy is intended to provide your creditors with as much repayment as possible while freeing you to begin rebuilding your life. There are different

kinds of bankruptcy for different situations, but they all have some things in common.

★ They all are handled in federal court.
★ They all require payment of case filing and administrative fees.
★ They all require individuals to receive credit counseling before filing.
★ They all distinguish between dischargeable and non-dischargeable debts.

Dischargeable and Non-Dischargeable Debts

A debt is discharged when it is eliminated and you are no longer responsible for it. The kinds of debts that can be discharged in bankruptcy vary according to which chapter you file under, but debts that are commonly not discharged include:

★ Child and spousal support
★ Income taxes
★ Student loans
★ Government fines and penalties
★ Secured loans
★ Restitution owed after a criminal conviction

DID YOU KNOW?

Credit card debit and medical bills are commonly discharged in bankruptcy.

Debts that commonly are discharged in bankruptcy include:

★ Credit cards
★ Medical bills
★ Unsecured personal loans

Your creditors will have the opportunity to object to having your debt with them discharged.

Types of Bankruptcy

All bankruptcy is not the same. It's important to know the options available so you can choose the type that best fits your current situation and goals toward financial freedom.

Chapter 7

Most individuals who file for bankruptcy file under chapter 7. Businesses can, too, but that's much less common, because this form requires the debtor to liquidate their assets to pay off as much debt as possible.

Once you file for bankruptcy you are assigned a case trustee, who will require you to provide certain documentation, including:

★ A list of your creditors, how much you owe, and for what
★ Information about your income
★ An inventory of your property and assets
★ A list of your monthly living expenses
★ Proof that you have had credit counseling, and any debt repayment plan that was created for you during counseling

While chapter 7 bankruptcy requires you to sell off assets, you don't have to give up everything you own. You're supposed to be getting a fresh start in life, and you won't get very far if you're left with nothing but the clothes on your back. Assets that are exempt from liquidation vary according to your state's laws, but generally speaking you'll be able to keep things such as:

★ Your home, assuming you can make your mortgage payments

DID YOU KNOW?

While chapter 7 bankruptcy requires you to sell off assets, you don't have to give up everything you own.

- ★ Reasonable household goods, furnishings, and personal effects
- ★ Your reasonably priced car
- ★ Your necessary clothing
- ★ Your pensions, if any
- ★ Tools and equipment you need for work

Nonexempt property that you will probably have to forfeit include such things as:

- ★ A second or vacation home
- ★ More than one vehicle
- ★ Collector's items
- ★ Cash, stocks, bonds, and other investments

Chapter 11

Individual debtors rarely file under chapter 11, the "reorganization bankruptcy." It is far more commonly used for businesses that need help restructuring their finances so they can keep operating. Once you file under chapter 11, creditors must stop trying to collect what you owe them while you figure out what you can do to get caught up. Your creditors will then vote on whether to accept your

reorganization plan. As long as it's reasonable, they are likely to do so—they know if you go with a chapter 7 bankruptcy instead, they could end up with nothing.

Chapter 13

A chapter 13 bankruptcy lets you keep your assets and come up with a plan to pay off your debts within three to five years. Unincorporated businesses can file under chapter 13 but that's unusual; it's much more commonly used by individuals with enough income to make it feasible.

Many people choose this kind of bankruptcy when their home is already heading into foreclosure—as long as they can get caught up on their mortgage payments, the foreclosure proceedings will stop. Chapter 13 bankruptcy will also give you a chance to come up with a new payment plan for other kinds of secured debts.

If your ability to keep up with your repayment plan is affected by circumstances beyond your control—if illness or injury keeps you from working, for example—you can ask the court for a hardship discharge. The court may agree to discharge the same kinds of debts that are dischargeable under a chapter 7 bankruptcy. Typically, a hardship discharge will only be granted if:

★ The reason you can't complete your plan is beyond your control and not your fault

★ You've paid your creditors at least as much as they would have gotten if you had filed under chapter 7

★ It isn't possible to modify your payment plan to make it work

How Long Does Bankruptcy Affect Your Credit?

Your credit score (learn more on page 63) is based largely on your history of paying your debts on time, so you'll take a hit if you file for bankruptcy. This is especially true if you file under chapter 7 and you have debts discharged without repayment.

A chapter 7 bankruptcy will stay on your record for up to ten years. Debts that were delinquent when you filed will stay on your record for seven years, just as they normally do. Debts that were not delinquent will fall off your report seven years after you filed.

A chapter 13 bankruptcy will stay on your credit record for seven years. Any debts that were delinquent at the time you filed under chapter 13 will fall off your credit report seven years later. Debts that were not delinquent will fall off your record when your bankruptcy does.

Rebuilding Credit After Bankruptcy

If your goal is to achieve credit invisibility (see page 66 for more details), you might choose to live debt-free after bankruptcy and wait out the years until your credit record is left with nothing to report. Life with poor or no credit can be frustrating and expensive, though, and most people will take the opportunity after bankruptcy to start rebuilding their credit. This takes time and patience, but it can be done. Financial advisors recommend that you:

★ **Check your credit reports regularly.** Make sure discharged debts show as discharged, and that those that were never delinquent are not so marked. Because negative activity falls off your record within specified periods of time (usually seven years), you'll want to make sure the dates of your bankruptcy filing and debt discharges are all correct.

★ **Apply for a secured credit card.** With this type of card, your credit line is equal to the amount of money you keep on deposit. It's kind of a credit card with training wheels—the lender does front you the money when you make a purchase, just as they do with an unsecured card, but they won't let you go over your limit. If you don't make your payments on time, they'll take it out of your deposit. You'll want to pay off the balance every month on a secured card as the interest is likely to be quite high, but that should be your goal in any case. Companies such as Capital One offer secured credit cards, and it's likely your own bank does, too.

★ **Apply for a secured or credit-builder loan.** As with secured credit cards, this kind of loan is based on money you keep on deposit. There are two kinds: either the loan is secured by money you already have in the bank, which you cannot access until you've paid off the loan, or the money the bank lends you is placed in a savings account that is yours after the loan is paid off. You're most likely to get this kind of loan locally, from a community bank or credit union.

★ **Ask someone with good credit to cosign a loan or credit card with you.** This won't benefit your credit score as much as a card or loan you get all on your own, but it will help. The cosigner shares responsibility for paying off any delinquent debt, though, so it's a big ask.

★ **Become an authorized user on someone else's credit card.** Again, this doesn't help as much as having your own card, but it can help a little. As when someone cosigns for you, adding you as an authorized user exposes the other person to risk—something not everyone will be willing to do.

★ **Make sure all positive information is reported to the credit bureaus.** Not every on-time payment you make is reported—for example, your rent and utility payments won't

> **GOOD FOR YOU!**
> Your landlord or utility companies may be willing to report on-time payments—to help rebuild your credit—if you ask.

show up unless you go to collections or get evicted. Your landlord or utility companies may be willing to report on your behalf if you ask, though. If they won't take the step, you have the right to add your own comments and information to your credit records (see page 67 for more on this route). This may or may not affect your credit score, but when a credit decision is being made by an actual person rather than a computer, it may help sway them.

Resources to Help You Bounce Back

You can find more information about filing for and recovering from bankruptcy from these sources.

US Courts

uscourts.gov

Discover all the information you need about the different types of bankruptcy, provided by US federal courts. Use the site's search function to get to "Bankruptcy Basics." You can also access bankruptcy forms to review and get started.

NerdWallet

nerdwallet.com

NerdWallet makes its money when you apply for products and services it recommends, but you don't have to buy anything to take advantage of its in-depth financial advice—including how to rebuild credit after bankruptcy. A search for "bankruptcy" will bring up hundreds of articles.

Take Control of Final Resting Decisions

Have a picture in your mind of how after-death care works—with an outrageously overpriced casket, an embalmed and cosmetically enhanced body, and a pricey burial in a commercial cemetery? You should know that the law does not require any of this.

If you've already filled out, signed, and shared your advance directive (more on that topic on page 125) detailing what kind of end-of-life care you want, the next step in planning for the inevitable is to decide what you want done with your body when you die. The government's interest in and control over the disposition of your mortal remains may be much less than you imagine.

While a dead body is not property in the usual sense, legally it is property in that specific individuals are vested with the right to decide what may or may not be done with it. Laws and regulations vary from state to state but, generally speaking, you have first priority in deciding what you want done with your remains, as long as you make your wishes known ahead of time.

Otherwise, rights fall to your spouse. If you are not married, or if your spouse refuses to take

GOOD FOR YOU!

Make your wishes known ahead of time so you can have a say in how your remains will rest for eternity.

responsibility, rights may pass to your adult children, your siblings, your parents, and so forth, in order of their relationship to you. If there is no one who is willing to claim your remains and make the necessary arrangements, a local governmental body will, as a last resort, take over.

Know All Your Choices

You may well have a picture in your mind of how after-death care works, in which survivors visit a funeral home, pick out an outrageously overpriced casket, view the embalmed and cosmetically enhanced body, and proceed to a large established cemetery, where they stand around the open grave throwing handfuls of dirt onto that beautiful casket, soon to be out of sight and moldering underground.

Would you be surprised to know the law does not require any of this? Your right to choose how your body is disposed of is not absolute and must be balanced with the public interest in health and safety, but you have much more control over this part of your life than you may realize.

You Can Choose Your Burial Container

Your choice of burial container will depend on where you will be buried. In a home burial, or if you are interred in a "green" or natural cemetery, you may choose a simple shroud or biodegradable container. If you purchase a plot in an established cemetery, it may require you to be buried not just in a casket but also within a burial vault—a nearly indestructible sealed container that will keep the ground above the casket from sinking if the casket collapses.

You Can Choose Whether to Be Embalmed

Embalming, in which bodily fluids are replaced with various chemical mixtures, is intended to preserve a body long enough for it to be transported and viewed. Embalming delays but does not prevent the body's natural, inevitable decomposition. It does not sterilize the body or make it less of an environmental toxin. In fact, the substances, such as formaldehyde, used for embalming are more environmentally unsound than naturally decomposing organic matter.

Embalming is not generally required by law in any state. There are exceptions, of course, and embalming may be required if:

- ★ Burial will occur more than 24 (in some cases, 48) hours after death
- ★ The body will be transported across state lines or internationally
- ★ The body will be transported by a common carrier (by plane, for example)

Additionally, funeral homes may require embalming if the body is going to be publicly viewed.

You Can Choose to Have Your Funeral at Home

Regardless of where you are being buried, and even if you are being cremated, you can have your funeral at home. This, of course, requires buy-in from your family, who will be left with the responsibility of cleaning and dressing your body and arranging the service. This was once common in this country before after-death care became commercialized and removed from daily life, and is still common in many parts of the world.

Not all families will be prepared to handle this kind of hands-on care, but some find it a meaningful and healing part of the grieving process. A home funeral may be followed by a home burial, or by removal of the body to a cemetery or crematorium. Some states may require the involvement of a funeral director in home funerals.

You May Be Able to Be Buried at Home

If you have an interest in genealogy, you probably haven't had to go back many generations before finding ancestors who were buried in small family cemeteries on their own land. This is much less common now, of course, but home burials are still legal in most parts of the country. You may be required to jump through a few legal hoops, though, and if this idea appeals to you it's best to plan well in advance.

As you would expect, the laws around home burials vary by state. Three states—Washington, California, and Indiana—prohibit home burials altogether. It is legal to bury bodies on private property in the other states, although some states (currently Alabama, Connecticut, Illinois, Indiana, Louisiana, Michigan, Nebraska, New Jersey, and New York) still require the involvement of a funeral director in certain aspects of after-death care, such as filing the death certificate and transporting the body. Each locality that allows home burials will have some regulations to follow that may involve:

DID YOU KNOW?

Home burial is legal (with some local regulation) in all but three states.

★ The minimum amount of acreage required
★ The maximum number of bodies that may be buried
★ How far the burial must be from any water source
★ How far the burial must be from property lines and/or city limits
★ How deep bodies must be buried

Establishing a Family Cemetery

Some states only allow burials in established cemeteries, but you may be able to establish a family cemetery on your private land. You may be required to perform a survey of the land you intend to use for the cemetery and submit it to the appropriate city or county government, then report all burials to authorities. Zoning regulations may apply, and if you ever sell the land the cemetery is on, you will have to disclose details to the buyer. It is illegal everywhere to disturb burial grounds, and any development, subdivision, or improvements to the land may require the remains be exhumed and reburied elsewhere.

You Can Choose a Disposition Other Than Burial

Buying a burial plot in an established cemetery continues to be an option, but you also have a growing number of alternatives.

Natural Burial

It's possible to enjoy a traditional ground burial and be environmentally conscious—you can choose a natural or "green" burial. This kind of interment eschews embalming as well as fancy caskets, opting instead for biodegradable shrouds or containers. Your body may be buried closer to the surface to maximize decomposition processes, and your final resting place may be marked with a found stone or with flowers or a tree, rather than an engraved tombstone.

Cremation

Cremation has become an increasingly popular method of disposition. It's cheaper than burial, doesn't require purchase of a casket or burial plot, and provides a relatively small amount of remains (known as "cremains") that can easily be stored at home or scattered outside. Cremation takes place in a special furnace that can achieve the very high temperatures needed to burn off the body's soft tissue. The bones left behind are then ground down into the smaller bits we think of as ashes. Despite the benefits of cremation, the release of persistent pollutants into the environment from crematorium emissions is a cause for concern.

Alkaline Hydrolysis

Alkaline hydrolysis uses water, alkaline chemicals, heat, and pressure to speed up the natural decomposition process. The end result is bone fragments that are ground up just as they are after cremation, and a sterile liquid that can be discharged into wastewater systems. Alkaline hydrolysis is considered more environmentally friendly than flame cremation but is not legal in all states.

Sea Burial

Federal law allows anyone to be buried at sea, as long as certain requirements are met. For example, the burial must take place at least three nautical miles from shore in water that is at least 600 feet deep (or 1,800 feet deep in some areas), no plastic may be involved, and the body or casket must be properly weighted to keep it from rising to the surface. You don't have to get a permit beforehand, but you do have to notify the Environmental Protection Agency (EPA) within thirty days of performing a sea burial. Burial in other bodies of water, such as rivers, lakes, and bays, are regulated locally and may be illegal.

DID YOU KNOW?

Federal law allows anyone to be buried at sea, as long as certain requirements are met.

Composting

In 2021, Washington became the first state to legalize human composting, or "natural organic reduction." In this process, the body is placed in a special container along with wood chips and microbes that help speed the process. Oxygen and, if needed, solar heat, are used to maintain a conducive temperature. The resulting compost can be used just like the kind you make in your backyard from yard debris and kitchen waste.

Body Farm Donation

Sky burial, in which a body is left out in the open, subject to weathering and animal predation, is not legal anywhere in the United States. If this kind of disposition intrigues you, though, you might consider donating your remains to a body farm. Technically, these facilities are known as outdoor forensic anthropology research laboratories. They study the decomposition of human bodies under various environmental conditions, insights that help forensic investigators establish time and manner of death when bodies are discovered under suspicious or unknown circumstances. Body farms are also used for cadaver dog training. Keep in mind, though, that you won't qualify for body farm donation if you die with certain communicable diseases.

Whole Body Donation

You may choose to donate your entire body for medical research and education. A number of facilities across the country accept donations, and acceptance and exclusion criteria vary widely. Some, for example, won't accept your body if you've donated any of your organs. Some require you to authorize the donation of your body ahead of time, and may allow your next of kin to refuse to hand you over. Many facilities will cover the cost of transporting your body and may also provide death certificates and cremation of your body after it has served its purpose.

You Can Choose to Have Your Cremains Scattered on Public or Private Land

All that is left after cremation are bone fragments, made up mostly of calcium phosphate along with a few other minerals such as potassium and sodium. There is no organic matter remaining, and so there is nothing that may transmit disease or otherwise contaminate the environment if the cremains are scattered outdoors, whether in your garden or in your favorite nature spot. As with everything else, laws about where on public property cremains may be scattered varies from state to state and federal properties have their own regulations, so check with the appropriate authorities ahead of time.

★★

Help or Hoax?
Six Feet Under

Must bodies be buried six feet underground? Not necessarily. Laws—which of course vary from state to state—specify how far underground the *top* of the body or container must be, usually between two and four feet. This is intended to ensure the decomposing body is deep enough to prevent transmission of disease, keep animals from smelling the body and digging it up, and prevent remains from working their way to the surface due to weathering. A typical casket is 16 to 24 inches deep, meaning **the depth of the grave may vary from about three and a half feet to six feet or so**. Proponents of natural or green burials advocate for shallower graves so there's more oxygen and microbial action to speed the decomposition process, as well as ensuring nutrients released as the body breaks down can reach trees and other vegetation at the surface.

Resources for Final Resting Rights

Although it's not something we tend to talk about every day, your resting wishes should be made clear ahead of time. These sources can help guide you through disposition decisions and how to document your choice.

Environmental Protection Agency (EPA)

epa.gov/ocean-dumping/burial-sea

The EPA website will tell you everything you need to know about sea burials.

Federal Trade Commission (FTC)

consumer.ftc.gov/articles/ftc-funeral-rule

The FTC Funeral Rule enumerates your rights to transparency about funeral costs, as well as clarifying which services and products you may choose from—or refuse.

Funeral Consumers Alliance

funerals.org/local-fca

This nonprofit organization protects consumers' rights to choose a meaningful, dignified, affordable funeral. It has local chapters throughout the United States that can offer you advice on home burials.

Green Burial Council

greenburialcouncil.org

The nonprofit council advocates for environmentally sustainable death care. You can learn all about green burial, how it works, why you might want to choose it, and where to find green burial–friendly funeral homes and cemeteries.

Nolo

nolo.com

Nolo has been publishing DIY legal information for forty years. Their website offers guidance on various aspects of end-of-life planning, including your rights regarding home funerals.

Stop the Tech Invasion

You can minimize the sharing of your private information and monitoring of your every movement while online. Take these simple steps to adjust your settings and habits—and protect yourself from spying eyes.

More than a decade ago, WikiLeaks founder Julian Assange called the internet the "greatest spying machine the world has ever seen." Since then, things have only gotten worse in terms of the internet's attack on users' privacy. First, companies and developers are constantly finding new ways to use our data against us. And then, of course, there's the government. After 9/11, their authority to monitor and investigate our computing habits has expanded far beyond what was comprehensible before that date. Here's how websites and apps track you, how your data can be used against you, and what you can do about it.

Who's Collecting Your Data?

Everyone wants to know where you're going and where you've been. What's the danger? You decide whether how other parties are using your information is legit based on the information in this chapter.

Social Media

Social media is arguably the ultimate privacy thief. Many people (voluntarily) share personal information on social media that they'd never consider disclosing in the "real" world.

Social media isn't free. The hidden cost is probably far beyond what you'd be willing to pay in fees to use a secure platform that protects its users. Social media sites use a process called data scraping to collect, arrange, and sell your personal information. They sell this information to advertising "partners" so companies can target you with ads for goods and services that are likely to interest you.

Then, there's the risk of data leaks. In-app messaging programs (learn more on pages 175–183), for example, are largely lacking in terms of privacy. If you use in-app messaging to communicate, remember that virtually anything on the internet is hackable.

Finally, if you're using social media, you should be aware that the government can use your online presence against you. In 2012, the courts ruled that a young man from New York lost all claims to privacy when he shared personal information with a friend through social media. The court ruled then that your "friends" or "connections" are entitled to take any information they have access to (about you) and share it with the government.

Additionally, there have been instances in which law enforcement officers and government agents have created fake profiles on social media to connect with and investigate people. No laws state they can only connect with suspects or known criminals, and there's nothing protecting the average Joe from this deceitful invasion of privacy.

Website Caches and Cookies

Caches store data about a website on your local network. While they're less of a hazard than cookies, caches can allow people on your device or network to check your browsing history, including which websites you've visited and when, and how much time you spent on each.

Cookies, on the other hand, store data about you. They store data about your habits, preferences, and personal information, such as usernames, passwords, and banking information. A website can use first-party cookies to store your information and browsing habits on their website. Third-party cookies are given or sold to advertisers and companies who can use your information to target you.

Medication Tracking Apps

Medication tracking apps can be handy if you take several medications or supplements and have trouble keeping them straight. However, when you download an app to your device, you're giving the developers access to your personal information and enabling them to link your activities within your app to your identity.

Medication apps are not regulated or protected under HIPAA or any health privacy laws. As a result, information from these apps is typically easily accessible to hackers who understand app development. Beyond that, if you don't lock your phone with a passcode, the information is accessible to anyone around you who may have malicious intentions. This is

DID YOU KNOW?

Medication apps are not regulated or protected under HIPAA or any health privacy laws.

especially problematic if you're taking controlled substances that might appeal to someone wanting them for their own use.

And there's nothing preventing law enforcement from accessing and investigating your phone if you're involved in a crime or an accident. For example, suppose you're involved in a car accident. Could law enforcement use your app data to suggest that the nonprescription sleep aid you use before bed could have affected your response time? It's impossible to say, but it's probably not worth the risk.

Fitness Apps and Wearable Fitness Trackers

The information users share with fitness apps is exceptionally personal. Height, weight, medical conditions, diet, sexual habits, sleep patterns, exercise regimes, and, perhaps worst of all, location data. While it's comparable to the information you'd share with your health care provider, the information you share with your fitness apps isn't protected under HIPAA.

In many cases, the data shared with fitness apps is public by default, but even if you've opted to keep your data private, your information is at risk. First, fitness apps, like many other mobile applications that are free or low-cost, make money by selling your information. Advertisers could use your lousy sleep habits to target you with ads for a new mattress, or your location information to target you with advertisements from a coffee shop along your running route.

Then, of course, any information stored digitally is at risk of hacking. Well-known apps have fallen victim to more than a few major privacy breaches. The risk is even higher if your app communicates via Bluetooth with a wearable tracker. See the tips and resources that follow for more information and guidance on health tracker privacy settings.

Period Tracking Apps

Millions of women use apps to track ovulation and menstruation. Unfortunately, these apps became exponentially more dangerous with the Supreme Court's 2022 decision to overturn *Roe v. Wade*, allowing states to criminalize abortion.

As with fitness data, developers can choose to share or sell the information you disclose through period tracking apps, and it's possible it could be obtained by law enforcement. You must consider how your data could be used against you if you ever seek access to abortion services. There are very real concerns that you could be prosecuted if data on your period app suggests you have conceived, but then you never have a pregnancy to show for it.

How to Protect Your Privacy

If you have an online presence and choose to disclose personal information in apps or programs, there's only so much you can do to protect yourself. Still, it's certainly better to take every possible precaution.

Set Unique Passwords

You should have no fewer than three unique passwords. If you're logging into your online banking using the same password you used for your first email address, it's time to reconsider. Choose at least three unrelated passwords that you can use for apps and websites with different levels of security: one for free  sites and apps that likely have minimal encryption, another for things like email where there's personal information but nothing too private, and a final, exceptionally complex password for things like online banking and access to security systems.

Always decline when a website asks if you want them to remember your log-in information. If you need help remembering your passwords, write them down (without context) and store the list in a safe place.

Best of all, use a password manager. A password manager, such as 1password (1password.com), will both generate strong, unique passwords for every account you have and store them so all you need to remember is a single log-in.

Sign Up with an Alias

There's no good reason to use your real name on any app or website where you don't really need to confirm your identity. When registering for something new, use a fake name or a nickname to protect your privacy. To keep it simple, you can use some variation or abbreviation of your name. If a site asks for your birthday, always go a day, a month, or a year off your actual date of birth. (Keep in mind, though, that providing inaccurate information in this way may complicate matters if you ever get locked out of an account and need to get back in. See Social Media, page 54.)

Create Different Email Accounts

The email address linked to your profile at your health-care provider's office should not be the same email address linked to your online casino profile. An inbox that houses confidential information will be more challenging to find and hack if you only use it for secure communications. Further, keep your personal and professional conversations separate, as any emails you send and receive from a work email address may be accessible by your employer.

Read Privacy Policies

The average privacy policy runs for thousands of words, but you should at least skim the policy when you sign up for a new product or service. If you can't commit, at least search the document (CTRL + F on a PC and Command + F on a Mac) for essential terms, including "third party," "share," "sell," "marketing," "encryption," and "stored."

Use the "Private Browsing" Mode

The private mode on your web browser can protect you in two ways. First, it prevents data about your browsing habits from being stored locally on your device or network. So if someone is snooping through your laptop to see what you've been up to, they'd have to dig deep to find anything about your activities while in private mode. Second, it hinders (but doesn't stop) cookies from being used to track you. If you're browsing in private mode, you're far less likely to see ads related to your history. However, the cookie protection isn't perfect, and you should still take other precautions.

Browse with a VPN

A virtual private network, or VPN, encrypts your data and reroutes it through a secure network. The rerouting process confuses the receiver and makes it more difficult for the receiving website or app to pinpoint precisely where the information is coming from. It's not the ultimate solution to your privacy concerns, and any information you share with the receiver will still be stored and processed according to their privacy policy. Still, a VPN is a

DID YOU KNOW?

Know the top six keywords to search for in privacy policies: "third party," "share," "sell," "marketing," "encryption," and "stored."

valuable tool in your privacy toolbelt, especially if you're concerned about location tracking.

Leave Your Fitness Tracker at Home

Don't wear your fitness tracker in crowded places. Tracking your workouts is one thing, but a crowded public space, such as an airport, is a prime spot for hackers to skim the data from your wearable using its Bluetooth connection.

Resources to Minimize Your Exposure

Online privacy concerns and wisdom for minimizing your risks pop up every day in all sorts of media outlets. At the time of publication, these sources offer some easy-to-implement advice.

Consumer Reports

consumerreports.com

Search "privacy + apps" for tons of information—including a look at various period tracker apps.

Federal Trade Commission (FTC)

consumer.ftc.gov/articles/how-protect-your-privacy-online

The FTC site has a section dedicated to online privacy and security. The article at the address above is a good place to start.

Wired

wired.com/story/health-fitness-data-privacy

This article will help you change your fitness tracker's settings to protect your personal information. The Wired website offers a whole section on security to explore.

Help or Hoax?

Google Yourself

It's not a bad idea to Google your name and see what connected information—such as your address, phone number, and other personal identifiers—it brings up. In fact, Google recently added a form through which you can request removal of false or explicit material related to your name or assets that put you at risk for identity theft, financial fraud, or other specific harm. But remember that Google is simply an index. **To truly clear your name, you'll need to contact the webmaster of the site where the content actually appears.** Your best bet: look for a "contact us" link or drill down to the site's hosting company to uncover a contact.

Credit Access

Guard Against Unnecessary Peeks

We haven't quite reached a dystopian state in which we are each assigned a number that indicates our value to society, but we are inching ever closer with a critical figure: our credit score. So, who should be allowed to know your number?

Calculated mysteriously, using secret algorithms no one can explain, your credit score will determine whether you can get a credit card or a car, home, or business loan and if so, how much it will cost you. If you do get that car loan, your credit score will affect your insurance rate. If you buy a home or rent an apartment, your credit score will help determine how much of a deposit you have to put down for utilities.

DID YOU KNOW?

If you prefer not to have a credit file available for others to peruse, it's possible to achieve "credit invisibility."

And a bad credit score may mean getting turned down for that apartment in the first place, as well as for the job you'll need to pay your rent. If you've made mistakes or suffered a run of bad luck that has lowered your credit score, the consequences may dog you for years.

Because credit scores are all about how you manage debt, if you've managed to live or become debt free it's possible to have no credit score at all. This is called "credit invisibility," and while it may complicate your life in some ways, if you prefer not to have a credit file available for others to peruse, it's possible to manage without one.

How Credit Scores Are Calculated

Credit reporting agencies are cagey about how they calculate their scores. You'll never know for sure how they came up with yours, but they generally consider:

★ Your payment history (whether you pay your accounts on time)

★ How many accounts you have

★ What kind of accounts you have

★ How long you've had your accounts

★ How much of your available credit you are using (your debt-to-credit ratio)

★ How often you apply for new credit

Who Invented Credit Scores?

The first business to come up with a credit scoring method was the Fair Isaac Company, and their system is known as FICO. Most credit bureaus use the FICO method, but some also use one from a FICO competitor called VantageScore.

What's a Good Credit Score?

What constitutes a good credit score varies according to the credit bureau and whether they use FICO or VantageScore methods, but scores usually range from about 300 to about 850. As a general rule:

★ Under 629 = Poor

★ 630 to 689 = Fair

★ 690 to 719 = Good
★ 720 and above = Excellent

Specialty Credit Reporting Agencies

The three big credit bureaus—Experian, TransUnion, and Equifax—focus on your use of credit. For other aspects of life, there are other smaller, more specialized agencies as well. According to the Consumer Financial Protection Bureau (CFPB), a governmental agency, these include:

★ Opening or using bank accounts (including bounced checks or overdrafts)
★ Apartment rental payments
★ Car insurance claims
★ Homeowners and renters insurance claims
★ Employment
★ Medical records or payments

Who Can See Your Credit Report?

There are legal limits to who can access your credit report, but the CFPB lists a number of businesses that can, including but not limited to:

★ Debt collectors
★ Lenders
★ Insurance companies
★ Employers
★ Banks
★ Utility companies

Freezing and Locking Your Credit

You can freeze or lock your credit file so that potential creditors can't access it without your express permission. This helps protect you from having someone else apply for loans or credit cards in your name, but it doesn't make your information entirely private.

Freezing Your Credit

You can freeze your credit by contacting each of the big national credit bureaus—Equifax, TransUnion, and Experian—online or by phone or mail. Freezing your credit is free and is recommended by many financial advisors as a way to protect yourself from identity theft and fraud.

Freezing your credit doesn't offer complete privacy or protection, though. For example, although no credit card company will issue a card in your name if they can't see your credit report, they can still look at it to see if they want to entice you to apply for one. Having a frozen file may complicate your interactions with the Social Security Administration, and you're likely to pay more for insurance if insurers can't check your file. To avoid problems like this, you'll need to thaw, or unfreeze, your credit record to allow access to it.

Locking Your Credit

In addition to credit freezing, each of the big three credit bureaus offers its own credit locking program. These programs may be bundled with credit monitoring services and may charge a fee. They may also be more convenient, giving you the ability to use the bureau's mobile app to quickly lock and unlock your credit as needed. As with credit freezing, credit locking helps protect you against certain kinds of identity theft and fraud but doesn't make your information entirely private.

Opting Out of Credit Prescreening

To stop credit card companies from prescreening you and sending you credit card offers in the mail, go to OptOutPrescreen.com. This is the official, government-sanctioned site for stopping these solicitations from showing up in your mailbox. You can choose to stop them for five years or permanently, and you can opt back in at any time.

Achieving Credit Invisibility

If you are "credit invisible," you have no credit history—or credit score—at all. Financial experts consider this to be a bad thing, and they are eager to counsel the credit invisible in how to go about building their credit. It's true that for most people, having a good credit score makes life easier in many ways, but if invisibility appeals to you it's possible to achieve it and to live a good life without credit.

First, Eliminate Debt

As long as you carry debt of any kind, you will have a credit record and a credit score (or scores). So if you are aiming for invisibility, you'll need to pay off and close any accounts you have. This is a project for the long run, because while negative credit items drop off your history in seven years, if you close an account that is in good standing it may remain on your record for up to ten years.

Then, Transition to Cash Payments

While businesses you already owe money to are required to accept payments in cash, private businesses may have the right to refuse cash for new transactions (see Legal Tender, page TK). Using a debit card gives you the best of both worlds—you can make cash transactions online or in person while still presenting the expected plastic card. Debit card activity isn't reported to the major credit bureaus but may show up with specialty reporting agencies, especially if you have a history of overdrawing your account.

Checking Your Credit Report

Federal law requires the big three credit bureaus to provide you a free copy of your credit report once each year, or any time you apply for credit and are turned down. Unless you have achieved credit invisibility, it behooves you to take advantage of your right to view your files each year, looking for errors or unauthorized activity.

You can request your annual report from each of the credit bureaus individually, but AnnualCreditReport.com has been authorized by the federal government to let you order reports from all three in just one place. You are strongly urged to avoid other websites that claim to offer this service, as they may be scams.

Disputing an Error on Your Credit Report

If you do find an error on your credit report, you'll want to take action right away, as correcting the

mistake can take time. It's recommended to contact the credit bureau directly, and each of the big three bureaus will have a process in place to handle disputes. Be prepared to prove your identity before they'll talk to you, and have any documentation on hand that, for example, proves you paid off an account showing as delinquent. You may also want to contact the company that submitted the erroneous information to see if they will make the correction from their end.

Adding Comments or Information to Your Credit File

Your credit file will contain information about you that has been submitted by third parties, generally your creditors—a case of someone else telling your life story. It may be possible for you to contribute to your story as well, either to add positive information or to dispute or comment on negative information.

Adding Positive Information

Not every account you have is reported to the big three credit bureaus. Utility companies, for example, don't usually report that you pay off your balance on time each month, nor do banks or credit unions report that you make regular deposits and never overdraw your accounts. Your excellent employment record and history of being an outstanding tenant are not likely to show up, either. You can ask the credit bureaus to add information like this to your file, although they aren't required to do so. If you are actively seeking financing or housing, you may find updating your current address, phone number, and date of birth to your file helps you in the short term, but carefully consider whether you want this information to become part of your permanent record.

DID YOU KNOW?

You have the right to add positive information and to explain negative information in your credit file.

Disputing or Explaining Negative Information

You have the right to add comments or statements to your credit file to explain negative information, whether general or account specific. Adding a note that you made late payments because you were preoccupied and forgot about them won't help you, but explaining that you were furloughed during the pandemic, were hospitalized, and saw your rent double overnight can give creditors insight into extenuating circumstances that were beyond your control. If you add account-specific information, remember that negative information drops off your report in seven years. You'll want to be sure to delete your explanation for late payments when the late payments themselves are no longer showing. The same goes for a general statement of explanation; you'll want to remove it once you're back on your feet and all your accounts are up-to-date.

Look Out for Credit Scams

As you seek to protect your credit, also protect yourself from becoming a target.

Credit Repair Agencies: Approach with Caution

A credit repair agency can help make sure your credit file is accurate and error-free, but it can't magically make negative information go away or guarantee to raise your credit score. Avoid any agency that demands money up front, promises unrealistic results, or tells you not to contact the credit bureaus yourself. The federal government provides a list of approved agencies (see Resources that follow), and it's a good idea to choose one of them.

Steer Clear of Credit Privacy Numbers

The other number that follows you through life, in addition to your credit score, is your Social Security number (SSN). It is intimately entwined with your credit file, as you will virtually always be asked for it when you apply for credit of any kind. The purpose of using your SSN in this way is to establish your unique identity, as there may be others with your exact name and even your exact date of birth.

If you have poor credit or want to keep your personal information under wraps, you may be tempted to obtain a credit privacy number (CPN), also known as a credit protection number or credit profile number. The idea is that you use the nine-digit CPN in place of your SSN any time your SSN is requested.

The problem with CPNs is that using one could land you in prison. They are often actual SSNs, taken from real people, which makes their use a form of identity theft. An entirely random CPN that is not associated with an actual person is unlikely to be accepted by any agency or company you try to use it with, and doing so may be considered fraud.

Resources to Secure Your Score

Check out these tools to avoid scams, protect your privacy, and take control of your credit status.

AnnualCreditReport.com

annualcreditreport.com

Go to this website to order your free annual credit reports. It's the only one authorized by the government and guaranteed not to be a scam.

Consumer Financial Protection Bureau

www.consumerfinance.gov/consumer-tools/credit-reports-and-scores

Learn more about your credit report, including how to dispute errors and how to improve your score. You can also find a list of all the specialty credit reporting agencies you didn't know existed.

Credit Bureaus

Equifax
equifax.com
800-685-1111

Experian
experian.com
888-EXPERIAN (888-397-3742)

TransUnion
transunion.com
888-909-8872

Credit Counseling Agencies

justice.gov/ust/list-credit-counseling-agencies-approved-pursuant-11-usc-111

If you decide to try a credit counseling agency, make sure you pick one that's approved and will get the job done.

IdentityTheft.gov

identitytheft.gov

Start here if you have been a victim of identity theft.

OptOutPrescreen.com

optoutprescreen.com

Register at this site to stop credit card company prescreening and solicitations, either for five years or forever.

DNA

Restrict Access to Your Records

Your DNA may be your most personal information. Know how to protect yourself from DNA being unlawfully used against you by insurance providers, employers, and law enforcement.

The explosion in popularity of direct-to-consumer DNA tests is largely due to a rising interest in genealogy. Many people want to know about their ethnic origins, who their ancestors were, and who makes up their current extended family. Of course, DNA analysis has many other uses as well, such as proving paternity and solving crimes.

Your DNA can reveal so much about you—your sex, your likely eye and hair color, your risk of developing chronic medical conditions such as diabetes, or inherited conditions such as Huntington's disease. It's important to consider the implications of sharing with unknown others what is perhaps your most intimate information.

Common Uses of DNA

Sharing your DNA is most likely to come into play in these four areas.

Genealogy

Companies such as Ancestry and 23andMe make tracing your ancestors, extended family, and ethnic makeup as easy as spitting into a tube and dropping it in the mail. These tests don't read your entire genome, but rather they look at specific points on your chromosomes that reliably estimate the degree of relation between two people. They also provide insight into your genetic makeup, giving you an idea of where in the world your ancestors came from.

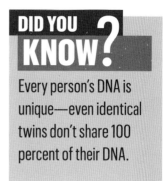

Paternity/Maternity

Paternity/maternity testing compares the DNA of two people to see if one is likely the parent of the other. Because genetics is much more complicated than just mixing the mother's DNA and the father's DNA and splitting it down the middle, this kind of testing can determine paternity/maternity with high probability that approaches, but does not quite reach, 100 percent. If you're just testing for your own peace of mind, you can buy tests to use at home. If you're testing for legal reasons, though, testing will have to be done at a clinic, hospital, or lab where the chain of custody can be maintained. Sibling DNA tests are also available; they are most accurate when parental DNA is factored into the picture.

Forensics

The DNA testing law enforcement relies on is nowhere near as fast and easy as it appears to be on television, but it has certainly become a critical tool for solving crimes when the identity of the perpetrator is unknown or in doubt. Every person's DNA is unique—

even identical twins don't share 100 percent of their DNA. As with paternity testing, forensic testing can't identify the owner of a DNA sample with absolute certainty, but it can show a match is close enough to have virtually no chance of having come from someone else.

Genetic Counseling

Many medical conditions can be passed down from parents to their children. Again, genetics is more complicated than just getting half of your DNA from your father and half from your mother—if that were the case, all siblings would be identical. Instead, each child receives a unique mix of their parents' genes, both good and bad. Genetic counseling can give a couple that is planning to have children a good idea of their likelihood of passing on inherited medical conditions.

The Genetic Information Nondiscrimination Act (GINA)

The Genetic Information Nondiscrimination Act (GINA) of 2009 was enacted to protect US citizens from discrimination in health insurance and employment based on results of DNA and other genetic testing. GINA provides a minimum level of protection; your state's laws may offer even more.

GOOD FOR YOU!

Under GINA, health insurers cannot require you to do any kind of genetic testing as a condition for getting health insurance.

Nondiscrimination in Health Insurance

Under GINA, insurers cannot require you to do any kind of genetic testing as a condition for getting health insurance. Should you volunteer any kind of genetic information, or if they happen upon it serendipitously, they can't use it to deny you coverage or charge you exorbitant rates.

★ Protections don't apply to life insurance, disability insurance, or long-term care insurance.
★ GINA doesn't cover routine lab results that might suggest you have or are at risk for developing a medical condition.
★ GINA doesn't apply to you if you have already been diagnosed with or started showing symptoms of a medical condition.

Help or Hoax?
Ancestry Research

Finding out about your genealogy can be very interesting, informative, and decently accurate. But there are some points to consider before spitting in the little tube and sending it off to that service.

★ **Hacking is not unheard of.** Although DNA data was not breached in this case, more than 92 million accounts from a DNA testing provider were found on a private server in 2017.
★ **Know what you're consenting to.** A majority of users give the required consent to share their DNA information with research partners. Although it could be argued that sharing the information helps advance science, carefully consider what boxes you're checking. If you've already opted in, you still may be able to ask to revoke that permission. Always re-review the privacy policy when you're alerted of changes made.
★ **Law enforcement has access.** Requests and subpoenas for data are happening.

Remember that a lot of this is still uncharted legislative territory; weigh the risks versus the benefits for you.

★ An insurer can ask for genetic information to determine whether and how much to pay for covered services. For example, if your policy covers mammograms at a younger age for those who are genetically at risk for breast cancer, they may ask for that information before they cover your early mammogram.

★ Not covered under GINA, because they have policies in place that offer similar protections, are:
- Members of the US military who receive their care through the Tricare military health system
- The Indian Health Service
- Federal employees who get care through the Federal Employees Health Benefits Plans

Nondiscrimination in Employment

Under GINA, employers may not require you to undergo any kind of genetic testing or buy your information from another source. If they do come into possession of any of your genetic information, they can't use it to make decisions about hiring, firing, or promoting you, or in any way treat you differently from others because of it.

★ GINA generally doesn't apply to companies with fewer than 15 employees.

   ★ GINA doesn't cover members of the military or federal employees, as they have their own policies.

   ★ It isn't a violation of GINA for your employer to obtain your family's genetic information indirectly, such as if you apply for extended leave to care for a sick family member. They still can't use that information to discriminate against you, though.

DNA Testing and HIPAA

The Health Insurance Portability and Accountability Act (HIPAA) was meant, as its name suggests, to make it easy to maintain health insurance coverage when moving from one employer to another. The part about keeping health information private wasn't considered a major part of the legislation, but it has become in many ways its defining feature.

Because the emphasis is on keeping health information secure as it is passed between health care providers and insurers, HIPAA only applies to certain "covered entities," including health-care providers, insurers, health-care clearinghouses, and business associates of those entities. This means Ancestry and other providers of direct-to-consumer DNA tests aren't subject to HIPAA—and neither are law enforcement agencies.

Law Enforcement and Your DNA

Law enforcement may come into possession of your genetic information in one of two ways: Either they take a DNA sample from you, or they access information that is provided by another source, such as a genealogy site or a health-care provider. Your rights in these two cases are very different.

DNA Samples Taken by Law Enforcement

The Supreme Court has ruled that taking a sample of your DNA after you've been arrested is no different from taking your fingerprints and photograph, and it is not considered to be any more optional. The most common method for obtaining the sample is to take a buccal swab, which painlessly collects skin cells from the inside of your cheek.

Your genetic information can then be compared to evidence found at the scene of a crime, and if it matches, can be admitted as evidence if you go to trial. If your charges are dropped or you are acquitted at trial, you can ask to have your DNA information removed from law enforcement databases; in some states, this may happen automatically. Laws and processes vary by state; see Resources that follow for an information source on state laws.

DNA Information Obtained from Other Sources

While the law around genetic information privacy is evolving, it seems pretty clear that the kinds of protected health information law enforcement can subpoena from health-care providers does not include anything related to DNA. The same cannot be said for providers and processors of direct-to-consumer DNA tests, such as those connected to genealogy sites.

Even if you don't submit your own DNA sample to one of these sites, if you've left genetic material behind for law enforcement to track down, they may do so through the DNA profiles of your relatives who have submitted samples. There's really nothing you can do about this, as you share DNA with numerous people you don't even know, any of whom may have genetic profiles stored in various online databases.

If you have submitted a DNA sample for testing by one of the genealogy sites, you can request they delete your information.

You'll need to check the website of each company to see how to do this.

Is DNA Admissible in Court?

DNA evidence is increasingly accepted and relied on to prove or disprove whether an individual has been involved in a given crime. The human genome is estimated to include at least 30,000 genes, though, and a forensic DNA analysis can't look at every single one of them. As with direct-to-consumer DNA tests, forensic DNA testing  compares genes at specific loci, or physical locations, within the DNA sample. The forensic analysis determines whether or not it is possible for the suspect to have left the genetic material found at the crime scene. The analysis yields one of three possible conclusions:

★ **Inclusion.** The DNA sample is included as a possible source of the genetic evidence. The genes at the examined loci matched, but that doesn't mean that every single gene in the individual's genome matched the evidence, as not all of them were compared.

★ **Exclusion.** The DNA sample is excluded as a possible source of the genetic evidence. The genes at the examined loci did not consistently match.

★ **Inconclusive.** The quality of the DNA sample wasn't good enough to make a reliable comparison, or some other complicating factor made it impossible to reach a conclusion (for example, more than one DNA profile was developed from the evidence).

Resources to Understand DNA Sharing Risk

Genetic Information Nondiscrimination Act (GINA)

ginahelp.org

Learn more about the protection GINA offers against genetic discrimination in employment and health insurance.

Lawfully Owed DNA

apps.rainn.org/policy/compare/lawfully-owed-dna.cfm

Check your state's laws on DNA collection, processing, and retention after arrest and after conviction.

Understanding DNA Evidence

ojp.gov/pdffiles1/nij/bc000657.pdf

This guide, designed for crime victims and those who advocate for them, provides a good overview of how DNA can be used as evidence.

Navigate Tickets, Tolls, Licensing, and Insurance

America is a big country, and Americans love to drive it. And it isn't just about getting from one place to another—as a popular 1980s car ad said, "It's not just a car, it's your freedom." But how much freedom do you have on the road?

If you're passionate about your personal freedom, you may not appreciate the government's efforts to limit and regulate your ability to drive when, where, and how you want. Many arguments have been put forth for why this kind of regulation is not legal or legitimate, and you may find these arguments compelling. Be aware, however, that those who rely on these arguments rarely, if ever, win in court.

Is There a Difference Between Traveling and Driving?

A popular argument for why you can't be required to get a driver's license to drive a private vehicle is that the Constitution guarantees every citizen the right to travel— a right that has been validated by numerous court rulings over the years. A driver's license, the argument goes, is

permission to do something you already have a right to do, and is therefore unnecessary.

But courts at every level (from circuit to Supreme) have repeatedly ruled that licensing does not in any way restrict the right to travel—without a license you are free to travel from one place to another, and one state to another, by any means other than operating a motor vehicle. The right to drive and the right to travel are not synonymous.

License and Registration, Please

The bottom line is that regardless of your sincerely held beliefs, flouting government regulations about driver's licenses, vehicle registration, and financial responsibility will have inevitable consequences should you get pulled over or involved in an accident. Only you can decide whether the risk is worth it.

Traffic Stops

A traffic stop is a kind of Terry stop (see page 30 for further discussion). The law enforcement officer must have an objective, reasonable suspicion that an infraction or crime is being committed, and the purpose of the stop is to investigate whether their suspicion was correct.
The stop can only last as long as necessary to conduct this investigation (checking your license and registration, for example) and take any directly related action, such as issuing a ticket.

What Are Your Rights?

You retain a number of rights during a traffic stop, but in the heat of the moment you and the officer may not see eye to eye on what those rights are. Should you have a difference of opinion, the time to challenge them is later, in court with an attorney, not on the side of the road with them standing over you with a hand on their sidearm.

★ You do not have to consent to a search of your vehicle. The officer may do so anyway if they have reasonable suspicion or feel it's necessary for their own safety.

- If you consent to a search, any evidence found may be used against you. If you don't consent and your vehicle is searched anyway, you may have grounds to challenge it later as an illegal search.
- According to the plain view doctrine, also known as clear view doctrine or plain sight rule, evidence of criminal activity that is clearly visible during a legitimate traffic stop—in the cup holder, for example, or on the back seat—can be seized. It is likely this will be considered probable cause to search the rest of the vehicle as well.
- If your car is impounded because you are driving while impaired, an inventory should be taken to ensure all your possessions are returned to you. Evidence found during this inventory may be used against you.

★ You have the right to record the stop.

★ You have the right to only be detained as long as necessary.

★ You have the right not to answer questions, especially if they are not directly related to the traffic stop itself.

★ You have the right to obtain the officer's badge number.

DID YOU KNOW?

You have the right to obtain the officer's badge number.

Staying Safe During a Traffic Stop

A traffic stop is just a moment in time, but it may have far-reaching effects on the course of your life. It's important to understand your rights, but also to remember you'll be in a better position to challenge police action later, when you're not in direct, immediate conflict with an armed officer.

If you are pulled over, for your own safety:

★ Turn off the engine.

★ Roll down your window.

★ Place your hands on the steering wheel.

★ Remain calm and nonconfrontational.

★ Calmly object to unreasonable questions or requests. If the officer is insistent, it's safer to comply, even if you disagree, and challenge the officer's actions later.

★ Exit the car if told to do so.

If You Are Armed

Laws about what to say if you are armed or have firearms in your vehicle during a traffic stop vary from state to state. If you carry firearms in your car, it behooves you to familiarize yourself with your state's laws. In any case, should there be any discussion of a gun in your possession, keep your hands on the steering wheel and ask the officer how they want you to proceed.

GOOD FOR YOU!

If you carry firearms in your car, familiarize yourself with your state's laws about what to say during a traffic stop.

Driver's License Laws

Every state requires you to have a valid driver's license in order to operate a vehicle on public roads.

Interstate Travel

Your driver's license must be issued by your state of residence. It is valid for driving in every other state, except that each state's minimum age, learner's permit, and age-related supervision laws apply. Should you move from one state to another, you will need to transfer your license to your new state of residence, usually within ten to ninety days.

License Endorsements

Driver's license endorsements provide additional privileges, such as the ability to drive a motorcycle or commercial vehicle. Criteria vary by state, but endorsements generally require a knowledge exam and a driving test, and you may have to take a specific educational course.

REAL ID

When you obtain or renew your driver's license, you now must choose between a regular license and a REAL ID–compliant license. For REAL ID, you will pay an additional fee and must provide additional documentation to prove your identity, your residence, and your citizenship.

REAL ID is optional, but as of May 3, 2023, you will need to present either a REAL ID–compliant license or another approved, trusted form of identification (such as a passport or military ID) wherever federal security measures are in place, including federal facilities and federally regulated commercial aircraft. This means your regular driver's license will no longer get you past the TSA checkpoint when you fly domestically.

Even though REAL ID is designed to comply with federal requirements, each state will continue to run its own driver's license program. According to Homeland Security, there will be no federal REAL ID database.

Enhanced Licenses

Some states (currently Michigan, Vermont, Minnesota, and New York) give the option of either Real ID or, for an additional fee, an enhanced license. Washington state offers only an enhanced license. An enhanced license is a "mini passport," as it allows you not only to fly domestically but also to enter the United States from Mexico, Canada, or the Caribbean by land or sea without a passport.

Do You Have to Buy Auto Insurance?

Every state requires you to prove financial responsibility—the ability to pay for damage you cause to others—in order to drive your car. Each state sets minimum amounts of damage you must be prepared to cover. There's no argument to be made that you shouldn't be held responsible for harm you cause to others, but there are different ways to go about it.

The most common way is to buy insurance from an insurance company. The cost depends on factors such as how much coverage is required and how solid your driving record is. Some states offer income-based low-cost insurance programs.

There are three alternatives to buying auto insurance.

DID YOU KNOW?

You have alternatives to buying auto insurance. Some states also offer low-cost programs.

Surety Bond

Your state may allow you to post a surety bond from a surety company. The dollar amount of the bond must meet the state's minimum coverage and works kind of like a line of credit. If you are found liable for injury or damage, the bond company will pay out up to the amount of the bond, and then you will have to pay the bond company back.

Cash Deposit with State

Some states allow you to deposit an amount of cash with the DMV that is equal to the minimum coverage required. In some cases, you can keep the money in a savings account assigned to the DMV.

Self-Insurance

Some states allow you to obtain a certificate of self-insurance, although you may still be required to post a surety bond or deposit money with the DMV. Self-insurance may be limited to businesses or to those with dozens of vehicles to insure.

What Are Your Rights?

If you get pulled over and can't show proof of insurance, you will probably get a ticket and a court date. It's possible to get a ticket dismissed or downgraded to a lesser violation, but you won't win by arguing you are exempt from insurance requirements. Penalties may include fines, having your car impounded or your license suspended, or even jail time.

DUI Roadblocks

Courts have held that the public danger from drivers impaired by alcohol or other drugs is so grave that the minor inconvenience of DUI roadblocks is reasonable.

What Are Your Rights?

Courts have also held that you have the right to avoid a DUI roadblock as long as you don't:

- ★ Fail to stop
- ★ Stop before the roadblock and switch seats with a passenger

★ Avoid the roadblock in a suspicious manner. It would not be suspicious, for example, to make a U-turn if in a place where U-turns are allowed, but it would be suspicious to make an illegal U-turn by driving over a grassy median.

Toll Roads

Roads are necessary for a functioning society, even for those who don't drive, so everyone pays for them through a combination of various kinds of taxes. Toll roads have an additional source of funding: fees paid by those who actually drive on them. Toll roads need to entice drivers, so they tend to be better maintained and offer more efficient travel than roads funded solely by taxes.

In the past, toll roads were fitted with toll booths, manned by people who could accept payments and make change. Eventually express lanes were added for those who did not need assistance in paying. The current trend is toward open-road tolling, or electronic toll collection (ETC), which eliminates the need for toll booths altogether.

With ETC, a transponder in your car transmits your information as you enter and exit a toll road, and payment is billed automatically. If you don't carry a transponder on these roads, your license tag is photographed and you are mailed a toll bill. The transponder option is more cost-effective and tolls billed this way are usually lower.

There's no getting around the loss of privacy that driving on this kind of road inevitably brings—your movements are going to be surveilled and recorded. As with any data collection system, the information recorded may be subject to hacking, and it's possible law enforcement could access your information as well. Your only option here, though, is to avoid these kinds of roads.

Parking Tickets

The busier and more overcrowded a city is, the more parking regulations you are likely to face. These regulations are intended to manage what may be a scarce public resource, and to keep people from parking in ways that endanger others. Of course, parking fees and fines also provide revenue for cities to help maintain parking infrastructure.

Some parking rules, such as how long you can remain in place and whether you need to pay, are communicated with signs and markings on the curb or pavement. Others, though, vary from one place to another and won't be signed or marked, such as how close to a corner you can park, or how far from the curb your wheels can be.

Whether through your own inattention or ignorance of local rules or through a lack of needed signage, you may at some point return to your car to find a ticket on your windshield. If you ignore the ticket, your fine will increase over time, and if you leave it long enough you may find yourself facing arrest, suspension of your driver's license, or towing or booting of your car.

Fvery municipality that issues parking tickets will have its own process for contesting those tickets, but it generally involves:

★ Submitting a statement explaining why you should not have been ticketed. You will usually have a deadline of three weeks or so to start this process, but in some places it may be as little as ten days.

★ Requesting an administrative hearing if the initial review doesn't result in the ticket being dismissed. You may have to pay the ticket in the meantime and wait for the fine to be refunded if the hearing goes your way.

★ Appealing the results of the hearing if your ticket is still not dismissed. Not every jurisdiction offers this option.

Resources for the Open Road

Minimum Car Insurance Requirements

nerdwallet.com/article/insurance/minimum-car-insurance-requirements

Find a summary of minimum insurance requirements in each state.

REAL ID

dhs.gov/real-id

Start here to learn everything about REAL ID.

Know What You Can Refuse on the Job

You can get the job, stay employed, or jump ship for the next great opportunity without compromising all of your principles and privacy. Here's how to gauge what an employer can get away with and where you can draw a line.

Whether you're applying for a new job, sticking with your current job, or planning to quit or retire, it's essential you understand what your (potential, current, or previous) employer can and can't legally do.

Before You're Hired

When you're in the job search and application process, it's tempting to say yes to any hoops and hurdles if you want the position enough. But you shouldn't have to give up all your personal protections to convince the employer that you're the right person for the job. In fact, poking and violating your privacy at this point is a red flag for how the employer may try to push the limits if you're hired. So what's legit and what's not as part of the candidate review process?

Running a Background Check

In some states, a potential employer can run a background check on you without your knowledge. Whether they do the check themselves or hire someone else to do it, a background check will typically involve searching public records to verify your identity, personal history, and credit rating, and to see whether you have a criminal record.

Typically, a background check is only legal if you've passed the initial phase of applicant cutting. In most cases, a potential employer isn't allowed to discriminate against an applicant based on information acquired this way. Still, the hiring process is subjective, and it'd likely be challenging to prove an applicant wasn't chosen because of something discovered on their background check.

To reduce the impact of negative past behavior, run a background check on yourself occasionally. Keep an eye out for incorrect negative information (which you'll need to formally dispute) and information that should legally be erased from your records. In some states, minor criminal activity should be scrubbed from a report after a specific time (typically seven years). Check your state's particular laws regarding reporting legal and financial mishaps.

Checking Your Internet Presence

Anything you share publicly on the internet is fair game when a potential employer is trying to decide whether you're a good hire. Unfortunately, some states have neglected to enact laws preventing employers from requesting an employee's username and password.

In general, it's a good idea to limit what you share about your life online. If you don't want to quit social media, set your profiles and posts to "friends only" to protect your privacy. If something damaging has been published online, you can request that the publisher remove the piece. If it's a matter of public record, though, there's not much you can do.

Fortunately, laws are in place to prevent employers from discriminating against potential or existing employees. So if an employer scanned your social media and found out about your religious affiliations, sexual orientation, or political beliefs, for example, it'd be illegal to discriminate against you based on that information.

Asking about Your Salary History

Many states have enacted salary history bans, which make it illegal for a potential employer to ask about your salary in past positions. However, if you disclose the information voluntarily, there's no law preventing an employer from using the information to set your salary in the new position. Keep in mind that asking about your salary expectations is not the same as asking about your salary history, and asking how much you expect to be paid is legal in every state.

If you live in a state that does have a salary history ban, you have the right to refuse to answer questions about your previous or current salary without repercussions. Otherwise, if you must discuss your salary, be sure to include compensation you receive over and above your base pay, such as overtime, benefits, and bonuses. If you're leaving your current position because you're not satisfied with the pay, be sure to tell them that. Also, discuss any additional

DID YOU KNOW?

Many states have enacted salary history bans, which make it illegal for a potential employer to ask about your salary in past positions.

expenses the new job will entail, such as increased transportation costs due to a longer commute.

Asking about Medical History or Conditions

The Americans with Disabilities Act (ADA) prohibits employers from asking certain medical questions, requiring a potential hire to undergo a medical examination, or asking for details about disabilities. However, an employer can make a job offer contingent upon a satisfactory medical report or exam. Still, it must be a company-wide policy, and all employees who work in the same position must undergo the same process and be evaluated in the same way. You can protect yourself by refusing to answer questions about your health until you've received a job offer.

Asking Any Questions to Estimate Your Age

The Age Discrimination in Employment Act (ADEA) protects job applicants from age discrimination, and a potential employer cannot ask any question to which the answer could be used to determine your age. If an employer asks, and you don't feel comfortable answering, keep it light by saying you've had time to develop as a person, you bring a unique level of experience to the company, and your age will not limit your ability to learn and grow within the company.

Asking about Family and Marital Status

Questions about kids and partners may seem innocent and friendly, but a potential employer may be using your answers to predict how reliable you'll be. It's illegal to ask about your family situation before offering you a job. It's illegal to discriminate against a

woman with young kids because of concerns about child care issues, for example, but that can be difficult to prove.

Protect yourself by politely declining to answer family-related questions. Instead, say something like, "I'm dedicated to keeping my personal and professional lives separate. Unless there's an unexpected and serious situation, such as a death in the family, I'm confident that my personal life will never affect my job performance."

After You're Hired

Once you're hired into a position, it's just as important to know your rights. What's permissible for your employer?

Requiring You to Work Overtime

Can an employer terminate you for refusing to work overtime? Unfortunately, yes. In fact, an employer can choose to terminate you for nearly any reason, as long as it's not discriminatory and as long as they provide you with sufficient notice and compensation. But you must be paid according to overtime laws, and you can't be forced to work so many hours that your health is threatened. If you feel you're unable to safely perform your duties in overtime, discuss your concerns with your employer. If you think you've been fired for refusing unsafe work, that's illegal and something you can pursue.

Asking about COVID-19 Vaccination and Requiring It

An employer can legally ask about your COVID-19 vaccination status without violating the Health Insurance Portability and Accountability Act (HIPAA). They can also require that all current employees get vaccinated, with exceptions for medical or religious reasons. If your employer requires COVID-19 vaccination and you're not comfortable getting the shot(s), try to compromise. You may be able to work from home or in a more private space, or carry out roles that aren't client-facing.

Forbidding Salary Discussions Among Employees

Under the National Labor Relations Act (NLRA), it's illegal for an employer to forbid employees from discussing salary, and it's unlawful to penalize them for doing so. You also have the right to use what you know about your colleagues' salaries to negotiate your own.

Turning a Blind Eye to Workplace Hostility

Employers are required to ensure their employees' workspace is safe, and they're legally required to take complaints and allegations of harassment seriously. The law extends beyond the workplace, too. Let your employer know if a colleague is harassing you outside of work. Once they know about the issue, your employer is legally obligated to work on a solution.

Offering Wellness or Healthy Lifestyle Incentives

Healthy, happy employees are typically more productive. But can an employer reward healthy behavior? The answer is complicated. An employer cannot legally withhold benefits or bonuses that other employees receive because you smoke cigarettes, consume alcohol, or use marijuana (if it's legal in your state). As long as your enjoyment of what some might consider vices is lawful, doesn't harm others, and doesn't affect your performance at work, what you do on your own time is your business. Any workplace wellness program should meet the following requirements:

★ Goals are scalable and reasonable. For example, an employer can't incentivize all employees to reach a BMI of thirty or lower within six months, or set a goal for all employees to run ten miles in ninety minutes by the end of the year.

★ Participation is voluntary. An employer cannot require that employees participate in a wellness program and can't penalize those who choose not to.

★ The program is safe and, if necessary, supervised by a professional.

★ No employees are discriminated against when setting a goal. If a goal doesn't suit a particular employee, they should set a different target with the same incentive.

After You Leave the Company

Laws vary by state, but restrictive covenants in employment, termination, or severance contracts typically hold up.

Requiring a Nondisclosure Agreement

In most cases, an employer can require that you sign a nondisclosure agreement. These types of contracts are usually intended to keep privileged information, such as trade secrets and client data, safe. However, there are some situations where an employer can't require you to sign a nondisclosure agreement. For example, it's illegal for your employer to demand that you keep quiet about abuse, harassment, or unsafe work practices.

Initiating a Noncompete Agreement

Noncompete agreements are not valid in some states. Further, unfair noncompetes are prohibited altogether. A noncompete agreement will only hold up if the employer can prove its conditions protect the company. For example, suppose you learned a confidential technique for achieving some sort of outcome. In that case, your employer could require you to sign an agreement stating that you won't accept a position with a direct competitor or start your own company using the same technique.

Restricting You from Taking Your Clients with You

In most states, employees are prohibited from taking a client list with them to a new company. In terms of taking individual clients, your employer can legally require you to sign a nonsolicitation agreement. Knowledge of your former employer's clients is confidential, and employers have a right to protect that knowledge through a nonsolicitation agreement.

Resources for Fair Employment

Noncompete Agreements

workplacefairness.org/non-compete-agreements

Get information about noncompete agreements from the nonprofit Workplace Fairness, which advocates for employees' rights.

Prohibited Employment Policies/Practices

eeoc.gov/prohibited-employment-policiespractices

Find out about the laws the Equal Employment Opportunity Commission (EEOC) enforces regarding employer requirements and practices.

Shield Yourself from Automated Identification

Throughout your day, your face and voice may be captured many times and linked to an identity— sometimes, not even accurately. But there are steps you can take to guard against misuse of the technology or mistaken identity.

Facial and voice recognition are two of the most common and invasive types of biometric recognition, which is essentially the automated identification of someone based on their biological traits—and yes, the process is just about as unsettling as it sounds.

Being tracked and identified by your voice or face is comparable to getting fingerprinted, having a mugshot taken, and your file added to a law enforcement database, except that you don't need to interact with law enforcement to be involuntarily subjected to biometric recognition.

What Is Facial Recognition?

Facial recognition is the capturing, assessment, and processing of the technical mapping of a person's face based on a photo or video. Facial recognition systems use algorithms to map specific characteristics of a person's face and identify the

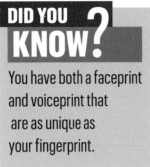
person. Converting the raw data into a usable form is a multistep process:

1. **Detection.** Motion, mechanical, or heat-sensing technologies alert the camera that there's a face visible. Depending on the setting, the sensors may detect many faces at once or catch just one.

2. **Capture.** The camera captures a photo or a series of photos (from a video) of the person of interest's face, typically from different angles and ideally with different expressions.

3. **Analysis.** Specialized software creates maps of the face that include topographical, size, and distance-based measurements. Points of interest include face length, distance between the eyes, lip contours, and more.

4. **Conversion.** The raw data is converted into a numerical representation, called a faceprint, that's as unique as a person's fingerprint.

5. **Comparison.** The faceprint is compared to all faceprints in the database.

Where Is Facial Recognition Used?

You likely meet facial recognition technology many times in your typical day.

Social Media

For years, Facebook stored data on more than a billion faces. However, they dropped their facial recognition system in 2021, likely in an attempt to regain the trust of their users after they made headlines for sharing users' data with an analytics firm.

After years of boasting about keeping users safe by opting not to use facial recognition software, Instagram (which, interestingly, is owned by Facebook's parent company, Meta) has recently started using the technology to verify the ages of their younger users. Teens may be asked to upload a photo of their ID and a video of themselves to prove their age and identity.

Home Security

Many home security systems are equipped with cameras with facial recognition software. Nest (owned by Google), for example, has a feature called "Familiar Face Detection," where it uses facial recognition to identify visitors and turns off notifications for the detection of frequent visitors. Older devices store facial recognition data on Nest's cloud-based system, while newer devices store it on (slightly) more secure internal memory.

Cell Phones

Modern smartphones use facial recognition to enable access. Some, including those that run on iOS and Android, use facial recognition to automatically tag and catalog photos in your digital library.

Airports

Long gone are the days of simply handing your ID or passport to an agent at the airport and having them look at you to make sure the ID or passport is yours. These days, you may self-scan at a kiosk and look into a camera that uses facial recognition to verify your identity.

DID YOU KNOW?

Any surveillance camera in a public space may be equipped with facial recognition software.

Public Spaces

Any surveillance camera (more on that topic on page TK) in a public space may be equipped with facial recognition software. Data collected through facial recognition and used by the government is perhaps the most problematic, as we're all already in their databases—they've had a photo of you since your first driver's license, passport, or other government-issued photo ID.

What Is Voice Recognition?

Like facial recognition, voice recognition software uses advanced technology to identify a person based on their unique characteristics—in this case, vocal quality and patterns. This is different from speech recognition, the technology used to transcribe speech or to understand commands (such as when you speak to your car's navigation system to ask for directions).

Voice recognition software collects, processes, and uses data similarly to facial recognition programs. Voice recognition relies on specific parameters, including intensity, pitch, volume, timbre, and dynamics, to create a voiceprint that, like a faceprint, is as unique as a fingerprint.

In text-dependent voice recognition, the software only analyzes how a person says a specific word or phrase. An example could be the keyphrase used to disarm an alarm once triggered.

Text-independent voice recognition is a little more complex and can be used to identify any person in any situation, regardless of what they actually say.

Where Is Voice Recognition Used?

You probably don't make as many phone calls these days as you used to, but no doubt you've called a business and heard an automated message telling you that your call may be recorded for quality control and training purposes. That sounds pretty benign, right? What you aren't told is that artificial intelligence (AI) may be used to analyze your recorded voice to gain insight into who you are and how you can best be manipulated. Once your voice has been captured, it may even be used to create a photo image of your face.

While voice recognition is most often used on phone calls, it can also be used in conjunction with the video from surveillance cameras to pin down your identity.

The Problems with Facial and Voice Recognition

With most new technology comes new problems. Biometric recognition technologies have been around for a while, but as they advance, they create expected and unexpected issues.

False Positives and Negatives

Imagine looking just enough like a known criminal to trigger an alert every time you try to enter a subway terminal or check in for a flight—that's a false positive identification. In contrast, false negatives are when a biometric recognition system fails to identify a person of interest, leading to a false sense of security. False outputs are rare, but they're more common in specific populations, which leads to the issue of racial profiling.

Outcome Reliability Inequality and Profiling

Because of the way it was developed, facial recognition technology is most accurate in identifying white men. People of color and women are significantly more likely to encounter a false positive or negative. Placement of the biometric recognition devices becomes a problem, too, when they're placed primarily in certain neighborhoods.

Protestor Identification

The First Amendment protects your right to peacefully assemble and protest. However, it doesn't protect you from retaliation from law enforcement if they can identify you through facial or voice recognition.

Accessibility

These advanced technologies aren't exclusively available to the government and police. There are plenty of AI-based facial recognition programs available to anyone with a computer, and some of them are even free. The availability of biometric recognition programs means that anyone can use your information against you, for whatever reason and to whatever end. Beyond that, all digitally recorded and stored data can be hacked. Your biometric data contains some very personal information and grants you access to things like bank accounts. Imagine what the right mind with the wrong intentions could do with that sort of power.

Privacy

And, of course, the ultimate concern with biometric recognition is privacy. In most cases, you don't opt into biometric recognition, and your data can be used without your knowledge.

Protect Yourself from Biometric Recognition

There are a few ways to protect yourself from the risks of biometric recognition.

★ Opt out of biometric processing at the airport and choose to verify your identity with a TSA agent instead.

★ Choose a pin code or password to secure your devices, rather than a face or fingerprint ID.

★ Use two-factor authentication on apps that use biometric recognition.

★ For important transactions, go to the bank in person instead of calling to confirm your identity.

★ Keep an ID on you at all times. If you're mistakenly identified, you'll want to be able to prove your identity without delay.

★ However you may have felt about wearing a face mask to prevent coronavirus transmission, one advantage you may have appreciated was the way masks can thwart facial recognition technology. You can protect yourself from biometric recognition by wearing a mask in public spaces.

> **GOOD FOR YOU!**
>
> Be patient and choose to wait in line for a TSA agent to personally verify your identity rather than giving your faceprint to a biometric processing kiosk.

Resources for Understanding Recognition Technology

Current and Planned Uses by Federal Agencies

gao.gov/products/gao-21-526

Read the US Government Accountability Office's 2021 report on the federal government's use of facial recognition technology.

New Biometric Updates

wired.com

Get the latest on where biometric recognition is being used (and sometimes banned) and advice from Wired tech experts on avoiding misuse of this technology. Search "facial recognition" and "voice recognition."

Speech2Face

speech2face.github.io

This presentation explains how a recording of your voice might be used to generate an image of your face.

Exercise Gun Freedoms Supported by Law

How much freedom do you have when it comes to purchasing and carrying a gun? That depends largely on where you live, but some gun rights are covered throughout the United States. Here are the firearm essentials to know.

Second Amendment rights have always been a hot topic in America, and never more so than today. Politics aside, no matter what your personal philosophy is on gun rights and safety, it's in your best interest to be familiar with your state's firearms laws.

Who Is Prohibited from Owning Firearms?

The federal Gun Control Act of 1968, codified at 18 U.S.C. § 922, generally prohibits the sale to, and possession of firearms by, anyone who:

- ★ Is under indictment for, or has been convicted in any court of, a crime punishable by imprisonment for a term exceeding one year (usually but not always a felony)
- ★ Is a fugitive from justice
- ★ Is an unlawful user of or addicted to any controlled substance

★ Has been adjudicated as a mental defective or has been committed to any mental institution at sixteen years of age or older

★ Is illegally or unlawfully in the United States

★ Has been dishonorably discharged from the armed forces

★ Has renounced their US citizenship

★ Is under a court order to restrain from harassing, stalking, or threatening an intimate partner or that partner's child

★ Has been convicted in any court of a misdemeanor crime of domestic violence

★ Intends to sell or otherwise dispose of the firearm or ammunition in furtherance of a felony, terrorism, or drug trafficking

★ Intends to sell or otherwise dispose of the firearm or ammunition to a prohibited person

Restoring Your Firearm Rights

If you lose your right to own firearms due to a criminal conviction at the state level, you may be able to petition the court to have your rights restored. If you are convicted of a disqualifying crime in federal court, though, you're likely out of luck—in that case, the only way to get your rights restored is to obtain a presidential pardon.

As you would expect, procedures for restoring firearm rights vary by state, but in every case you will have to have served out

your prison term, paid any related fines or restitution, and completed parole. There is often a waiting period of several years after meeting all these criteria before you can apply to have your rights restored.

Federal Firearms Licensing

You don't need a license to sell someone a gun from your personal collection now and then, but if you are "engaged in the business of dealing in firearms," you need to apply to the Bureau of Alcohol, Tobacco, Firearms and Explosives (ATF) for a federal firearms license. It doesn't matter if you have a bricks and mortar store or if you sell over the internet—if you repeatedly buy and sell firearms with the aim of making a profit, you are engaged in the business and must be licensed. Currently, dealing in firearms without a license may subject you to criminal prosecution with a potential sentence of up to five years in prison, a fine of up to $250,000, or both.

Although you can sell a gun if you're not running a business and don't have to be licensed, some laws still apply. For example, without a license you can't sell firearms across state lines—the only way to legally do so would be to engage the services of a licensed dealer to complete the transaction. Additionally, although you're not required to run a background check on the buyer, it would be illegal for you to sell to them if you knew, or had good reason to suspect, that they are prohibited by law from possessing firearms.

Background Checks

The National Instant Criminal Background Check System (NICS)

allows federal firearms licensees to initiate background checks on potential buyers, either directly with the FBI or through a contact in their state that accesses the FBI information.

To start the process, someone who wants to buy a firearm fills out an ATF form provided by the dealer. The dealer then transmits the information on the form to the FBI or to their state contact. Whichever way the NICS is accessed, it searches nationwide databases to see whether the buyer is on any list of persons who have been reported as ineligible to possess firearms.

If you are not a licensed firearms dealer you aren't required to run a background check before selling one of your own guns. If you would like to vet a buyer for your own peace of mind, though, you can pay a licensed dealer to run a check for you.

If You Are Denied by the NICS

If your NICS check mistakenly finds you ineligible to buy firearms, you can appeal your denial. How you go about appealing will depend on whether your background check was run directly with the FBI or through a state agency. See "NICS Participation Map" in the Resources section that follows for information on your state's level of participation with the NICS.

If you repeatedly run into problems with the NICS, you can apply for the Voluntary Appeal File (VAF). The FBI will do some research, and if it finds you are eligible to buy firearms in spite of the difficulty you've had getting approved (for example, if you are being confused with someone else with the same name), they will issue you a Unique Personal Identification Number (UPIN) that will expedite the approval process in future transactions.

Firearms Safety at Home

Federal law requires that licensed firearms dealers also have for sale secure gun storage or safety devices that are compatible with the firearms they sell. These are defined by ATF regulations as:

★ Devices that, when installed on a firearm, are designed to prevent the firearm from being operated without first deactivating the device

★ Devices incorporated into the design of firearms that are designed to prevent the operation of a firearm by anyone not having access to the device

★ Safes, gun safes, gun cases, lock boxes, or other devices that are designed to be or can be used to store firearms, and that are designed to be unlocked only by means of a key, a combination, or other similar means

Federal law does not require you to use secure gun storage or safety devices in your home, but many states do have such laws. In some states you must secure all unattended firearms, while in others you are only required to secure firearms if there are, or might be, children in your home. Depending on your state's laws, you could be held criminally liable if a child accesses a firearm in your home, even if they don't discharge it or cause any injuries. Be sure to research and understand the child access prevention (CAP) laws specific to your state.

GOOD FOR YOU!

Know your state's child access prevention laws—in some states, you must secure all unattended firearms whether there are children in the home or not.

Concealed Versus Open Carry

It's impossible to summarize current state laws on carrying firearms in public, as such laws are constantly changing and being updated. State law may allow you to carry a concealed weapon, with or without a permit, and with or without taking handgun safety classes. Some states that issue permits for concealed weapons recognize permits from other states, but not all do.

Some states allow you to openly carry firearms in public places for any reason, others only for some legitimate purpose, and still others never. Some states require a permit to carry a handgun, but do not require a permit to carry a long gun. If you want to take firearms with you as you move about your community, it behooves you to familiarize yourself with your state's current laws.

Resources to Strengthen Your Firearm Knowledge

Federal Firearms Law

govinfo.gov/content/pkg/USCODE-2011-title18/ html/USCODE-2011-title18-partI-chap44- sec922.htm

Get the full text of the federal law on sales and possession of firearms.

Firearms Laws by State

atf.gov/firearms/state-laws-and-published-ordinances-firearms- 34th-edition

This Bureau of Alcohol, Tobacco, Firearms and Explosives (ATF) page provides links to the firearms laws of every state.

Help or Hoax?
The Best Carry

People often hold strong opinions on which carry method is safer and more useful, but both come with pros and cons. Base your decision first on laws where you live and then your own personal comfort.

Concealed Carry Pros
* ★ Less likely to be stopped for questioning by law enforcement
* ★ Less likely to upset people who are fearful of firearms
* ★ Less likely to be targeted by a "bad guy with a gun"

Concealed Carry Cons
* ★ Weapon is harder to access in an emergency
* ★ Hard to conceal a weapon in hot weather clothing

Open Carry Pros
* ★ Weapon is readily accessed in an emergency
* ★ May deter "bad guy with a gun" from acting
* ★ Not affected by weather

Open Carry Cons
* ★ Likely to be stopped for questioning by law enforcement
* ★ May cause public panic, especially in light of frequent mass shootings
* ★ Easier for someone else to access your weapon

National Instant Criminal Background Check System (NICS)
fbi.gov/services/cjis/nics

The FBI runs this system that is used for background checks of potential firearms buyers.

NICS Participation Map

fbi.gov/file-repository/nics-participation-map.pdf/view

See your state's level of participation with the NICS.

Open Versus Concealed Carry States

https://worldpopulationreview.com/state-rankings/open-carry-states

https://worldpopulationreview.com/state-rankings/concealed-carry-states

See maps of the current available (2022) open and concealed carry laws, with a summary of which states require permits.

Don't Give Up Your Location Data

Chances are, you have at least one tracking device on you right now that's transmitting location information to everyone from individuals and companies to governmental agencies. Ready to thwart the spying?

The vast majority of us are walking around with small tracking devices (cell phones) in our pockets or bags at all times. And you know those edge-of-your-seat scenes in action movies where the feds try to keep the caller on the line for a certain amount of time to pin down the caller's location? Not entirely accurate. Cell phones transmit location data constantly. If that's not enough, individuals, companies, and agencies can also gather location data from your car, the photos you post online, and, in some cases, standalone trackers that they've hidden among your belongings.

Ways You're Being Tracked

It doesn't take a spy or detective, like in those old movies, to follow you. Here are the most common methods both government and nongovernmental agencies use to gather your location data.

Your Cell Phone

This is the big one—the popular portable tracking device that many of us voluntarily carry around. Unless your location services are switched off (and, in some cases, even if they're switched off—more on that to follow), app developers, companies, and government agencies can acquire data from your phone.

★ **Tech companies,** such as Google, use cell phone location data to determine how much traffic is on a particular route, how busy a store is at any given time, how much time people spend (on average) at a certain location, which ads to show you, and more.

★ **Your home security company** uses your phone's location data to determine whether you're home or away, most significantly in the event of an emergency or a crime.

★ **App developers** use your phone's location habits to target you with personalized ads (or to sell the information to companies who may target you with personalized ads).

★ **An employer** may use your company phone's location data to find out when you arrived at work, when you left, and whether you took a few extra minutes for lunch.

★ **A scorned lover or stalker** who once had access to your phone may use it to track your movement.

★ And finally, **police or government agencies** can use your phone's location to place you at a crime scene or to track your movement if they suspect you're engaging in some sort of illegal activity.

Your Vehicle

Cartapping is an invasion of privacy through your car's onboard computer systems. If your vehicle is equipped with a connectivity system, the government can get a warrant for access to the data collected through that system. This may include location information, details on driving habits, and even audio recordings.

If you drive an older vehicle with no connectivity or GPS equipment, information about your location and driving habits may still be accessible to anyone who can get close enough to your car to attach a physical tracking device.

AirTags

There are many types of GPS trackers, but Apple AirTags are widely available, inexpensive, and easy to conceal. About the size of a large coin, an AirTag can be placed just about anywhere—it would take mere seconds for someone to drop one into your bag or to stick one onto something you own—and it can be set up off-site. In addition, most portable tracking devices, including AirTags, run on a battery and can transmit data for up to a year without requiring a new one.

Metadata

Image metadata is essentially a text description of the conditions surrounding the creation of a photographic image. Metadata includes information that is of interest to professional photographers, such as focal depth, aperture, and shutter speed, but it also

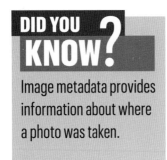
provides information about the photographer, the date and time the photo was captured, and where it was taken.

★ If you're a suspect in a crime, the police will use metadata from your phone, camera, or online photos to understand your recent activities and behaviors.

★ Apps and companies may use metadata to learn more about you and target you with unsolicited information or ads.

★ And, most alarmingly, the metadata attached to your photos online opens up the door to anyone online who may have dodgy intentions.

How to Protect Yourself from GPS Tracking

If you don't want to share your every move, here are some ways to sidestep the tracking or at least make it more difficult.

Make Cell Data More Private

You won't be able to prevent cell phone tracking entirely. Even if you disable location services on your phone, the government can ascertain your approximate location through cell tower triangulation, where they analyze the communications between your phone and three or more nearby cell towers. However, there are steps you can take to protect your privacy to some degree.

If Your Phone Runs on iOS
Go to Settings > Privacy > Location Services, and turn off Location

Services. Before you do, though, scroll down to see which apps have been using your location data. Scroll all the way to the bottom of the page to find out what the different icons mean.

If Your Phone Runs on Android

Open Settings > Connections or Privacy (depending on your device) > Location. Here, you can switch off location services. You'll also see a list of apps that have recently used your location data.

Downgrade Your Car Connectivity

It may seem unreasonable, but buying an older vehicle without connectivity features is the best way to ensure you don't fall victim to cartapping. If a more aged, low-tech vehicle doesn't meet your needs, consider canceling your connectivity subscriptions (OnStar and SiriusXM, for example, have both been ordered to provide location data to feds in the past). You can also have some of your car's connectivity features professionally removed by an automotive technician.

Search for Auto Trackers

A GPS tracker can be hidden inside or outside your car. To search your vehicle for unwanted and unauthorized trackers, focus on the interior first, as it's a little less labor-intensive to check around inside than to roll up under your vehicle.

★ **Check the onboard diagnostic II (OBD II) port first.**
  Mechanics use this port, typically located around the bottom of the dash or steering wheel on the driver's side of the vehicle, to diagnose problems when you bring the car to the garage.

It's a common location for GPS trackers, as plugging a tracker into this port allows the device to collect data on location, speed, mileage, and more. If you don't own a diagnostic scanner or some other device that you've personally plugged into the port, the port should be empty. Anything connected to the port you didn't connect yourself should be considered suspicious.

★ If there's nothing plugged into your car's OBD II port, **proceed to check the whole interior.** In the light, perform a visual search of the car's interior (front, rear, and cargo spaces). If you don't see anything unusual, perform the same search in the dark and look for blinking lights.

★ **Next, move on to the exterior.** Most exterior trackers are hidden in easy-to-reach areas, so you won't need to (and shouldn't, unless you're a qualified mechanic) move anything around. Instead, using a flashlight and a mechanic's mirror, check areas near the car's perimeter for anything that seems out of place. Pay close attention to the wheel wells, as they're common hiding spots.

★ If you've thoroughly swept the inside and outside of your car and haven't found a tracker, that doesn't necessarily mean you're in the clear. If you're still uneasy after a visual search, **consider investing in a bug detector**. Keep in mind that some GPS trackers only transmit (and are only detectable) while the vehicle is moving, so you may need to enlist help and have a passenger sweep the car while you're driving.

Finally, if you're still worried you're being tracked but your search has been fruitless, you'll need to hire a professional. An automotive technician specializing in electronics will have access to special tools and the knowledge to assess your car's wiring for signs of tampering (which may indicate that a tracker is attached somewhere).

How you disable an automotive GPS tracker will depend on how it's connected to your car. If it's plugged into the OBD II port, you can disable the tracker by simply unplugging it. If it's a battery-operated tracker attached to your vehicle with automotive tape, you can gently pull on it (applying heat with a hairdryer may loosen the adhesive) and destroy or dispose of it. Disconnecting a tracker that's wired to your car will be more challenging, and you should hire a professional automotive technician to take care of the removal. If you tamper with the wires, you'll risk causing a short circuit, which can be costly to fix.

Uncover AirTags

Apple is trying to combat the issue of AirTag stalking by alerting people with iPhones if a tracker is nearby for an extended period. Of course, this doesn't help people with non-iOS phones or no phone. Apple has developed an app for Android users (Tracker Detect on the Google Play Store), but if your phone runs on a different mobile operating system or is not a smartphone, you may need to get creative.

★ **Assess possible hiding spots.** If you believe a tracker may be hidden in your coat or a handbag, physically check the item for signs of tampering or for a rigid spot that seems out of place (GPS trackers are typically made of hard materials, such as plastic).

★ Some people report they've had success finding a hidden AirTag using a Bluetooth scanner, but reviews are mixed.

If you have access to a Bluetooth scanning device or app, it's probably worth a shot, but keep in mind that they're not entirely reliable.

Should you find an Apple AirTag hidden in your belongings, the easiest way to disable it is to remove its battery. First, flip the AirTag so it's metallic side up. Then, press down on the Apple logo and turn the metallic face counterclockwise. Once you hear a "pop," you'll be able to remove the face and the battery.

Remove That Metadata

Before you post a photo online or share it through a messaging app, take a moment to strip the location metadata.

On Your PC
Navigate to the file folder, find the file, and right-click. When the menu pops up, click Remove Properties and Personal Information. From there, you can create a copy of the file with all metadata removed or choose which data to eliminate from the original file.

On Your Mac
Open the image you want to strip in Photos. Click Image (in the top menu) > Location > Hide Location.

On Your Android Phone or Tablet
Open Google Photos and tap the "i" icon to check for metadata. If your photos are tagged with location information, you'll need to install a third-party app to remove it. You can search the Google Play Store for "metadata remover" or "EXIF remover" to find a trustworthy app with good reviews. Install the app and follow the in-app instructions to remove the metadata from your photos.

On Your iPhone or iOS Tablet

Open the Photos app and navigate to the Library tab. Tap the photo you'd like to remove location data from and tap the "i" icon at the bottom of the screen. Next, locate the map and location data, and click Adjust. Finally, tap No Location to remove the location information.

Resources for Keeping Your Location Secure

AirTags and Unwanted Tracking

apple.com/newsroom/2022/02/an-update-on-airtag-and-unwanted-tracking

See what Apple is doing to mitigate this issue.

Photo Location Privacy

consumerreports.org

Consumer Reports is looking out for you. Search "EXIF" for more information about what data photos may reveal.

Health-Care Decisions and Directives

Choose What's Best for You and Your Family

If you are reading this book, you know you want the freedom to live your life your own way. But have you thought about what it means to maintain your personal autonomy through to the end of your life?

There may come a time when hard decisions have to be made about your medical care—what kind of care you should receive, how long it should be continued, whether it should be discontinued. That time may not necessarily be far in the future, at the end of a long battle with a terminal illness. It could come today, as the result of an accident or a medical emergency such as a stroke or heart attack.

Right now—while you are fully in control and able to communicate your wishes—is the time to think about the care you want if you are severely ill or injured. You also need to think about who you want to speak for you if you are unable to speak for yourself.

Studies show that having an advance health care directive greatly increases the likelihood you will receive the care you want—and be spared any efforts you don't want—in an emergency or at the end of your life. Yet two-thirds of American adults have not taken this simple step to look after their own interests.

DID YOU KNOW?

Two-thirds of American adults have not prepared an advance directive to communicate their health care wishes.

What Is an Advance Health-Care Directive?

An advance health-care directive is sometimes popularly referred to as a "living will." It's a document you prepare that states what kind of medical care you want or don't want—at any time, really, but especially if death is possible or inevitable, and especially if you are incapacitated and can't communicate your wishes.

Regardless of the terminology used, there are three distinct parts to ensuring your end-of-life care wishes are known and, as much as possible, adhered to. Sometimes these parts are broken down into separate documents, but in most cases all three steps are combined into one.

Making Decisions about Medical Care

This is the basic purpose of an advance directive: deciding what kind of medical care you do or don't want at the end of your life or if you are unlikely to have any kind of meaningful recovery (if you will remain in a persistent vegetative state, for example).

Forms vary from state to state, but generally you may choose to have:

★ Every available life-sustaining treatment
★ Limited life-sustaining treatment, such as artificial feeding and hydration
★ No life-sustaining treatment of any kind
★ Decisions about life-sustaining treatment made by your health-care proxy

Designating a Health-Care Proxy

A proxy is a person who is authorized to act on behalf of another person. In this context, your proxy is a person designated to advocate for you in the event you are unable to do so for yourself. This can be anyone you choose, as long as they are at least eighteen years of age. The authority of your health care proxy takes priority over that of anyone else, including your spouse.

It's important to keep in mind that no matter how comprehensive your advance directive, you can't foresee every possible decision that will have to be made if you need medical care while you are incapacitated. Having a designated proxy means someone who knows you and knows how much your autonomy means to you can help direct your care.

The form for designating a health care proxy may be incorporated into an advance directive or may be a separate document. In many states the person you choose must sign the form to indicate they are willing to serve as your proxy. Not everyone is willing to take on this responsibility, and even someone who is willing may not be available or able to do so when needed, so it's a good idea to designate one or even two alternative proxies.

Granting Power of Attorney for Health Care

Whereas an attorney at law is licensed to represent others in legal matters, an attorney in fact is anyone who is authorized to act on behalf of another person—very similar to a proxy, and in the health-care context the terms may be used interchangeably. The biggest difference between them is that power of attorney may also be given for other purposes, such as managing your financial affairs.

You will often see this document referred to as a *durable* power of attorney. The "durable" part means it takes effect only when you are incapacitated and unable to direct your own care. The designation of a health care proxy and the granting of durable power of attorney for health care are usually combined.

What to Do with Your Advance Directive

★ Give a copy to your health-care provider(s).
★ Give a copy to your designated health-care proxy.
★ Give a copy to anyone else who might be called on to produce your directive, including your close friends, family members, clergy, or attorney.

★ Take a copy with you if you are admitted to a hospital or care home.
★ Keep a copy in your handbag, backpack, briefcase, and/or glove box.
★ See whether your state offers an advance directive registry.

What to Know about Advance Directives and Proxies

Here are points to keep in mind as you work through your decisions and documents for the first time or review your directives and proxies—as you should every year or two.

You Don't Need an Attorney

You may want to consult with an attorney to have your questions answered, but you don't need an attorney to complete the forms for an advance directive or health care proxy. You can pick up the forms from your health-care provider or download them from various websites and fill them out yourself.

You Do Need Witnesses or a Notary

Most states require you to have two witnesses when you sign your advance directive, a few (currently, Missouri, North Carolina, South Carolina, and West Virginia) require you to sign before a notary, and some (such as Oregon) allow you to choose between witnesses and notarization. Generally speaking, your witnesses may not be anyone involved in providing your health care and may not be your designated health-care proxy. Your chosen proxy may have to accept their designation in writing.

You Can Revoke Your Advance Directive

You can change your mind about your advance directive at any time. As long as you are mentally competent at the time you are receiving (or refusing) care, you can simply say you want something other than what is in your directive. Otherwise, the revocation process may differ from state to state. It may be enough to retrieve any copies you have given out and destroy them, but you may need to formally revoke the directive in writing. Signing a new directive will automatically revoke any previous directive.

GOOD FOR YOU!

To find out whether your state has a registry, just search the internet for "advance directive registry" and the name of your state.

Divorce Will Remove Your Spouse as Your Proxy

If you have designated your spouse as your health-care proxy, ending the marriage will automatically revoke their standing. If you still want your ex to be your proxy, you'll need to go through the designation process again.

Some States Have Advance Directive Registries

Many states have established registries that will store your advance directive for easy access. They may charge a small fee and may provide a wallet card showing where your directive is registered and how to see it. To find out whether your state has a registry, just search the internet for "advance directive registry" and the name of your state.

Another State Might Not Honor Your Advance Directive

Generally speaking, any other state will honor the advance directive you have completed in accordance with your home state's laws. This may not always be the case, though, so if you spend much of your time in more than one state (if you live in Connecticut and work in New York, for example), consider filling out a directive for each state.

Your Choices May Conflict with Law or Providers

Depending on your state and the facility in which you receive care, your wishes may not be carried out exactly as you choose. In some states, for example, if you are pregnant, life-sustaining treatments will not be withheld or withdrawn until after your pregnancy ends, whether your baby survives or not. Advance directives are not legally binding, and there is always a possibility a health-care provider will feel your directions conflict with their own personal values or are medically inappropriate; this may set up a conflict with your health-care proxy, and your care may have to be transferred to another provider.

Your Written Advance Directive Is Not Enough

An advance directive can be destroyed, misplaced, or ignored. Proxies may be unavailable to take part in care decisions. You should still have an advance directive, of course, and should share it with your family and health-care providers. However, you should also openly discuss your philosophy and wishes with those closest to you. Whether you want everything done, nothing done, or something in between, make sure they've heard you say so out loud—you never know when this might be the deciding factor.

Help or Hoax?
A Health-Care Proxy for Your Child

As your child gets older, your access to their health records and ability to make health-care decisions for them will change. Parents are usually considered to be their minor child's health-care representative, with full access to their medical records and the ability to direct their medical care. In some states, though, once a minor is permitted by law to independently consent to medical care, their information is protected under the Health Insurance Portability and Accountability Act (HIPAA). In any case, once your child turns eighteen, HIPAA will provide them complete privacy, and they may want to designate you as their health care proxy. If your child is incapacitated and needs medical care while away at college, for example, **health-care providers may give great weight to your preferences on your child's treatment, but being designated as their health-care proxy will ensure you have the ability to make critical decisions.**

Should You Agree to Be a Health-Care Proxy?

Just as you should carefully consider who you want to ask to be your health-care proxy, you should think carefully before agreeing to be a proxy for someone else. Reasons to consider declining include:

★ You have trouble making decisions.

★ You and the other person have very different beliefs about end-of-life care.

★ You would be uncomfortable following the person's wishes if their family members disagreed.

★ You would be unable to make the decision to end care ("pull the plug").

★ You live far away or would frequently be out of the area.

★ You don't feel close enough to the person or feel you know them well enough.

Myth: Advance Directive Is the Same as DNR

An advance health-care directive spells out what kind of life-sustaining medical care you do or do not want if you are near death or unlikely to recover consciousness. This kind of directive generally addresses treatments and procedures such as intubation, intravenous (IV) fluids, dialysis, and feeding tubes.

A do not resuscitate (DNR) order—also known as a do not attempt resuscitation (DNAR) order, a no code order, or an allow natural death (AND) order—addresses what should or should not be done if your heart stops beating or you stop breathing. Resuscitation involves any procedure intended to restart your heart or restore breathing, such as:

★ Chest compressions and rescue breathing (cardiopulmonary resuscitation, or CPR)
★ Application of electrical shock (defibrillation)
★ Drugs such as epinephrine and atropine

While you can complete and sign your advance directive yourself, a DNR is a medical order that must be signed by a physician, nurse practitioner, or physician associate (formerly known as a physician assistant). A DNR order may be placed in your medical record while you are a patient in a hospital or care home.

If you are not a hospital patient or care home resident, you may be able to obtain an out-of-hospital DNR order. In this case, a special bracelet, pendant, or wallet card can ensure your wishes are followed in the event of an emergency—paramedics, for example, have to attempt resuscitation unless they have good evidence you have a DNR order in place.

In some states you may be able to include a DNR order as part of your advance directive, but often it is a separate document.

Resources for Health-Care Control

CaringInfo
caringinfo.org
CaringInfo is a program of the National Hospice and Palliative Care Organization, which is a membership organization for hospice and palliative care providers. Its website offers advice on how to talk with loved ones about your or their end-of-life care, information about different kinds of care, and links to advance directive/health-care power of attorney forms for each state.

Department of Veterans Affairs

va.gov/find-forms/about-form-10-0137

Download a PDF advance directive that can be filled in digitally and then printed, or printed out and then filled in.

My Directives

mydirectives.com

On this site you can fill out a digital advance care directive or upload one you've already completed. Your document will be stored in the cloud, where it can be readily accessed by anyone you give access to, including participating hospitals, eliminating the need to carry or produce a paper copy of your directive. You can update your document at any time and even add a video statement if you wish. There's even an iPhone app that puts your information in front of your lock screen so it can be easily accessed in an emergency, wherever you are.

Five Wishes

fivewishes.org

Five Wishes offers advance directive forms and guidance for a fee. Directives can be filled out digitally but are not stored in the cloud for remote access.

 HIPAA

Understand How Far Your Privacy Protection Goes

You may be more discerning with the personal health information you share when you realize how little is covered under HIPAA and how many loopholes in the protection there are.

HIPAA stands for Health Insurance Portability and Accountability Act (1996). Enforced by the US Department of Health and Human Services (HHS), HIPAA generally protects disclosure, access, and use of your protected health information (PHI) without your consent.

HIPAA does not cover every single instance of anyone discussing any aspect of your health information.

HIPAA was meant to make it easy to keep your health insurance coverage if you change jobs. The HIPAA Privacy Rule wasn't the main focus of the legislation, but PHI protection is what HIPAA is best known for now.

HIPAA emphasizes keeping health information secure as it is passed between health-care providers and insurers, and so it only applies to certain "covered entities," including health-care providers, insurers, health-care clearinghouses, and business associates of those entities. It does not cover every single instance of anyone, anywhere, ever asking questions or discussing any aspect of your health information.

What Information Is Protected by HIPAA?

HIPAA's Privacy Rule protects "individually identifiable health information" in the possession of any covered entity (more on that to follow) or its business associates, and applies to electronic, paper, and oral records.

Individually identifiable health information is any information that directly identifies or provides enough detail for the identification of the individual (name, address, date of birth, Social Security number, and so on) and relates to their:

★ Past, present, or future health condition (mental or physical)
★ Access to health services
★ Past, present, or future payment for health care received

HIPAA does not protect "de-identified" health information in which identifying details have been removed or were never connected, and that offers no reasonable means for identifying a person.

Where Does HIPAA Apply?

HIPAA applies to "covered entities." These include:

Some Health-Care Providers

HIPAA-bound health-care providers include doctors, psychologists, dentists, chiropractors, pharmacists, nursing home and clinic operators, and other professionals who transmit private health information electronically. However, a provider who uses

technology such as email but doesn't communicate private health information electronically is not covered.

Health Plan Providers

Health plan providers are insurance providers that offer individual or group health, dental, vision, and prescription drug coverage. Medicare, Medicaid, Medicare+Choice, Medicare supplement insurers, and long-term care insurers are also health plan providers.

There are two types of government-funded programs that don't qualify as health plan providers in this context:

1. Programs whose primary purpose is something other than paying the cost of health care (the food stamps program, for example, is not a health plan provider)

2. Programs whose primary purpose is directly providing health care or making grants to fund the direct provision of care

Health-Care Clearinghouses

Health-care clearinghouses are entities that process private health information and may include health management information systems, value-added networks, and companies, organizations, or individuals who offer billing or repricing services.

Business Associates

Business associates are any individuals or organizations that require access to private health information to carry out a task on behalf of the covered entity. Examples include organizations that offer data analysis, utilization review, billing, or claims processing.

Exceptions to the Privacy Rule

There are exceptions for persons and organizations covered under the definitions of "covered entities" just discussed. The HIPAA Privacy Rule allows—but does not require—the use and disclosure of private health information when it is believed personal privacy is balanced by public interest. These twelve instances are known as national priority purposes:

★ Required by law, if demanded by way of a statute, regulation, warrant, or court order

★ Public health activities if requested by:
  - A public health authority who is authorized by law
  - Entities whose activities or products are FDA-regulated for purposes of adverse event reporting or tracking, post-market surveillance, or product recalls
  - Individuals who were or reasonably suspect that they may have been exposed to a communicable disease when authorized by law
  - Employers, when the information is necessary to comply with Occupational Safety and Health Administration (OSHA) processes

★ Health oversight activities including monitoring and assessing health-care plans, policies, benefits, and providers

★ Victims of abuse, neglect, or domestic violence, to facilitate investigation or ascertain a conviction in an abuse, neglect, or domestic violence case

★ Judicial and administrative proceedings, if requested through an administrative tribunal

- ★ Law enforcement, as evidence in a crime, or to identify or track a victim, suspect, or missing person
- ★ Functions concerning the deceased, to identify the deceased person or to determine the cause of death
- ★ Organ or tissue donation, to facilitate the process of organ or tissue donation
- ★ Research, if any (not all) of the following conditions are met:
  - A waiver is granted by the appropriate governing body (Documented Institutional Review Board [IRB] or Privacy Board)
  - Limited data is provided
  - The information is essential in preparing for research
  - The information will be used solely for research of descendants and the information is necessary for research

HIPAA Misconceptions and Failings

HIPAA compliance programs cost billions of dollars annually to sustain, and who covers the bulk of the cost? Taxpayers, of course. But that's not even the biggest issue with HIPAA. The major concern with the Act is that many people believe the HHS has broad reach to enforce the protection of private health information and that any person or organization that leaks information, whether intentionally or unintentionally, is subject to prosecution. That couldn't be further from the truth.

HIPAA Is Not the Hippocratic Oath

Many believe that HIPAA protects the information they share with their doctor or other health care providers, but unfortunately that's not necessarily the case. The rules and regulations on this are very unclear, and there's a lot of room for interpretation.

If you thought patient-doctor confidentiality was addressed by HIPAA, you might have been thinking of the Hippocratic Oath, which is not a law but a code of ethics that physicians swear to. The oath states in part that "Whatever I see or hear in the lives of my patients, whether in connection with my professional practice or not, which ought not to be spoken of outside, I will keep secret, as considering all such things to be private."

Health Apps Aren't Covered by HIPAA

The average person probably shares more personal health information with their cell phone than with their health-care provider. The personal information you share with and store in health tracking apps such as fitness trackers, menstrual cycle and fertility apps, medication trackers, and mental wellness apps is not covered by HIPAA except when you transmit the data stored in them to a covered entity. The companies that offer these apps can use your information pretty much as they please—read each app's privacy policy for more details.

HIPAA Doesn't Apply to Schools and Employers (in Most Cases)

Schools and employers handle loads of personal information about their employees and students, from vaccination records to doctor's notes to information about absenteeism. Unfortunately, none of that information is protected under HIPAA because the schools and employers are not covered entities.

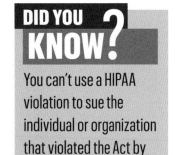
HIPAA Can Limit Your Access to Your Health Records

No one wants to face a fine for a HIPAA violation, so clinics and health care providers are extra cautious about releasing medical records, even to patients. It's likely, for example, that if you request a copy of your lab results or appointment notes, your provider will require that you pick it up in person. While HIPAA doesn't restrict the discussion of medical information by phone, many providers are hesitant or don't fully understand HIPAA and won't accept the risk.

Patients Can't Sue for HIPAA Violations

HIPAA violations are penalized with fines levied by the government and may be considered fireable offenses by some covered entities. But you can't use a HIPAA violation to sue the individual or organization that violated the Act by sharing your information, and you can't use it to seek compensation.

HIPAA and Reproductive Health

In the wake of the US Supreme Court's 2022 decision to overturn *Roe v. Wade* and allow states to criminalize abortion, it's essential to understand that HIPAA will not protect you if prosecutors demand access to your reproductive health records. "Required by law" is the first of the twelve national priority purposes for which HIPAA privacy protection laws are waived. As a result, law enforcement agencies can gain access to your reproductive health records, regardless of how your health-care provider collects and handles the data.

HIPAA and Gender-Affirming Care

Some states have taken action to label the provision of gender-affirming care to minors as child abuse. The HHS Office for Civil Rights has clearly stated that the PHI of those receiving gender-affirming care is protected under HIPAA.

Other Protective Health Laws

HIPAA is not the only health law that exists to protect you in a health care setting. Your state may have its own regulations in addition to the following federal laws.

Patient Safety and Quality Improvement Act (PSQIA) 2005

The Patient Safety and Quality Improvement Act (PSQIA) was enacted to encourage health care providers to report conditions at their facilities that may endanger patients. All information provided by health-care whistleblowers for this purpose is kept confidential. To maintain patient privacy, the HHS fines anyone found responsible for leaking a patient's protected information.

Americans with Disabilities Act (ADA) 1990

The Americans with Disabilities Act protects all disability-related health information collected by an employer, including medical exams required to start or resume a job and any medical information voluntarily disclosed as part of a corporate health program.

Resources to Understand HIPAA's Reach Versus Limits

Health Insurance Portability and Accountability Act of 1996 (HIPAA)

congress.gov/bill/104th-congress/house-bill/3103

You can read the full Act here.

US Department of Health & Human Services

hhs.gov/hipaa/for-individuals/index.html

Get the facts—including your rights under HIPAA, how your information may be used or shared, and how to file a complaint if you think your rights were violated—directly from the government agency that polices HIPAA.

Centre for International Governance Innovation (CIGI)

cigionline.org/articles/putting-our-bodies-online-the-privacy-risks-of-tech-wearables

CIGI offers a deep discussion of tech wearables and their privacy risks. Hint: They're not covered under HIPAA.

End the Neighborhood Tyranny

Fly that flag! Hang out clothes in "right to dry" states. Fight to change rules that make no sense. You have options even when you're living in an HOA community.

If your home is your castle, it's the last place you expect to have someone else telling you how to live. But property anywhere may have deed restrictions attached, and if you purchase a home in a common interest community or development, you may be subject to any number of rules, regulations, and restrictions imposed by a homeowners association, or HOA.

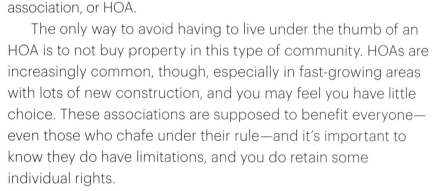

The only way to avoid having to live under the thumb of an HOA is to not buy property in this type of community. HOAs are increasingly common, though, especially in fast-growing areas with lots of new construction, and you may feel you have little choice. These associations are supposed to benefit everyone— even those who chafe under their rule—and it's important to know they do have limitations, and you do retain some individual rights.

What Is a Common Interest Community or Development?

In a common interest community or development, you own your home but also share common areas and facilities with your neighbors, ranging from sidewalks to pools. Everyone is billed fees, or dues, to help maintain the common interests. These fees are subject to change as costs increase, and special assessments may be levied for unexpected expenses such as storm damage.

What Is a Homeowners Association?

Every common interest community will have a homeowners association, with members usually elected during an annual meeting of homeowners. The HOA is expected to be run democratically, with changes to rules voted on by all homeowners and determined by majority rule.

The generally accepted purpose of an HOA is to maintain property values. Common areas are maintained by the HOA to ensure they are well kept up, and residents are subject to rules about what they can and cannot do with their individual properties.

There is no solid evidence, however, that homes subject to HOAs increase in value at a higher rate than those without them, and in some cases they may lag behind. One possible reason is that buyers who strongly value their individual rights don't want to be governed by their neighbors and will buy elsewhere.

Your Homeowner Rights

HOAs do have a lot of power, but they are supposed to operate for the benefit of the community and individual homeowners. As a homeowner and an HOA member, you have the right to:

- ★ See all HOA documents, including financial statements and vendor contracts
- ★ Question fees and special assessments, and ask to have them justified
- ★ Not be discriminated against on the basis of your race, color, sex, religion, national origin, familial status, and/or disability
- ★ Add a ramp, keep a service animal, or otherwise accommodate a disability
- ★ Vote for board members, run for board membership, and attempt to remove board members from office
- ★ Install a satellite dish and solar panels
- ★ Display a US flag

Additional rights you may or may not have include the right to:

- ★ Hang your clothes outside to dry (if you live in a "right to dry" state)
- ★ Grow a pollinator-friendly garden and/or native plants instead of grass
- ★ Display political signs

Some HOAs Are Voluntary

In many communities, joining and being subject to the rules of the local HOA is not optional, no matter how you feel about it. Sometimes, though, joining the HOA is voluntary. This may be the case if the HOA was created after the community had already been established and not everyone agreed to it, or because the founders simply chose not to make it mandatory. Voluntary HOAs may be called community or neighborhood associations. They have the same goal of protecting property values, but also look to encourage a sense of community and keep the neighborhood safe and livable. You can obviously choose not to join a voluntary HOA or neighborhood association.

Can You Refuse to Join a Mandatory HOA?

If you buy property in a common interest community or development that has a mandatory HOA, you won't have the option of refusing to join. Payments may be due monthly, quarterly, or annually, and are usually paid directly to the HOA rather than being included in your mortgage payment. However, you may be able to include your HOA dues with your house payment and have your lender deposit the funds into an escrow account for later payment to the HOA (this is the same way lenders handle property taxes and homeowners' insurance premiums).

What If You Don't Pay HOA Fees?

If you don't pay your HOA fees, the HOA board will likely take increasingly punitive measures, such as:

★ Demanding payment
★ Suspending your community privileges, such as use of a pool or fitness center

- ★ Filing a suit against you in small claims court
- ★ Sending your past due bill to a collection agency
- ★ Placing a lien on your property
- ★ Foreclosing on your home

The bottom line is that mandatory HOA dues are an inescapable part of your housing cost in this kind of community, and refusing to pay them could cost you your home. If you don't want to be subject to an HOA, don't buy property in this kind of community.

Taking Action Against HOA Rules

HOAs are governed by an elected board of directors made up of local residents. If you live in a community with an HOA, there are measures you can take to protect your rights and have a say in the rules you have to live by.

Run for Board Membership

Check your HOA's bylaws and your state's laws to see whether there are any special requirements you have to meet before you can run for a spot on your HOA's board—in some cases there are few, if any. Typical requirements include:

- ★ Must be a resident or property owner
- ★ Must not be behind in any HOA payments
- ★ Must not be in litigation against the HOA
- ★ Must not be related to anyone on the board
- ★ Must not have any felony convictions

In some cases you can nominate yourself for board membership, and in others you must persuade someone else to nominate you. Either way, to win you'll need the votes of a majority of your neighbors, so you'll want to start planning ahead to make yourself known (preferably in a good way) and familiarize yourself with your HOA's rules and management responsibilities.

Change the Rules—or Board Members

HOA rules and regulations are not written in stone, and they can be changed if a majority votes to do so. Check your HOA bylaws to see if there is a specific process for making changes, whether it involves starting a petition or just showing up at a meeting to propose the change.

If the board is resistant to change, you may want to focus on replacing its members with more like-minded people. Again, the process will vary but will involve either recalling a sitting member or promoting a rival when a member comes up for reelection.

Dissolving an HOA

Laws vary by state, but it may be possible to dissolve an existing HOA if enough residents agree to it. The dissolution process may be long and expensive, though—it isn't the kind of project you'll want to undertake unless you know you want to stay in your home for a very long time.

Resources for Protecting Your Rights

Legal Rights of Homeowners in HOA Communities

hoamanagement.com/homeowners-rights-against-hoa

HOA Management offers a roundup of individual rights in HOA communities and answers frequently asked questions—including how to fight an HOA stipulation.

Opposing Your HOA

wikihow.com/Fight-Your-HOA-(Homeowners-Association)

Although not official legal advice, this article provides possible steps you can take to fight an HOA and helps you understand the dynamics involved in dealing with such a board.

Over-the-Air Reception Devices Rule

fcc.gov/media/over-air-reception-devices-rule

Learn about your right to satellite dishes and solar energy systems.

Take Advantage of the Law's Shelter

As an American, you enjoy the presumption that you are a peaceful, law-abiding citizen. If you find yourself involved in a trial as a jury member or defendant, here's what you need to know about the jump to a guilty verdict.

You are free to go about your business without being harassed by law enforcement. If anyone wants to say otherwise, it's up to them to provide convincing evidence that you've done something wrong. This is what's known as the presumption of innocence, often stated as "innocent until proven guilty."

If you're charged with a crime and go to trial, the judge or jury must decide whether the prosecutor has proven, beyond a reasonable doubt, that you are guilty of the crime. Although you would probably want to make a convincing case for your innocence, that isn't actually your responsibility—it isn't up to you to prove you're *not* guilty.

What Is Reasonable Doubt?

If you've ever watched a trial, either real or fictional, you've probably had a gut feeling about whether the accused was guilty or not. If you serve on a jury, though, your gut feeling isn't enough.

Your job is to look at the evidence you've been given and decide whether it is sufficient to convince you the defendant is guilty as charged.

To doubt something is not the same as knowing or believing it isn't true—the essence of doubt is that you don't know whether it's true or not. A reasonable doubt is one that is based on reason, not on feelings or intuition. If the evidence provided at trial comes up short and leaves you not knowing whether the accused is guilty or not, you have to decide on a verdict of "not guilty."

"Not Guilty" Versus "Innocent"

In court, the opposite of *guilty* is not innocent—it is *not guilty*. Even though we talk about the presumption of innocence, unless you were there when the crime was committed (in which case you would not be serving on the jury!) you can't say the defendant is *innocent*. You can only say that the prosecution has not proven its case beyond a reasonable doubt and you cannot say, based on the evidence presented, that the accused is guilty.

Bench Trial Versus Jury Trial

If you are charged with a crime, the Constitution gives you the right to be tried before a jury of your peers, or social equals—people who are enough like you to understand your circumstances and motivations. This right isn't absolute, though; the Supreme Court has ruled that you only have the right to a jury if your charges are serious enough—generally, if your conviction could result in a custodial sentence of more than six months. State laws

differ, though, and you may be entitled to a jury trial even if you are facing a shorter sentence.

For less serious crimes, you may be tried in front of a judge in what is known as a bench trial. In a bench trial, the judge will not only rule on matters of law but also take on the jury's role in deciding whether or not you have been proven guilty. In some cases, you may be able to waive your right to a jury and choose a bench trial instead, as long as the judge and the prosecution agree.

Why would you want to give up your right to a jury trial? You might expect a judge to be more neutral, to understand complex evidence without having to be walked through it step by step, and to understand what aspects of your history are and are not relevant to the matter at hand. A bench trial is likely to go much faster than a jury trial and be far less costly for you. On the other hand, a judge may have their own biases, just like any other person, and that may work against you.

Your Right to an Attorney

The Sixth Amendment gives you the right to legal counsel if you are charged with a crime. It's well established that this counsel is so critical to ensuring due process (as required by the Fourteenth Amendment) that it must be provided regardless of your financial situation. This is the part of the Miranda warning that says, "If you cannot afford an attorney, one will be appointed for you." A government-appointed attorney is known as a public defender.

Like many other rights, though, the right to an attorney is not absolute. The Supreme Court has ruled that while you always have a right to a public defender if you are charged with a felony, you won't necessarily get one if you are facing a minor charge and incarceration is not on the table.

If your state's public defender program is underfunded, the attorney you are provided might not be a very good one. If you go to trial with a public defender and are convicted, you might be able to argue their poor representation, known as ineffective counsel, was responsible for your conviction. This can be hard to prove, but if you are successful you are likely to be granted a new trial.

Presumption of Innocence Must Be Explained to the Jury

The Supreme Court has ruled that to ensure a fair trial, the judge must instruct the jury that the default setting for the person sitting before them is that they are innocent of any crime. They must be reminded that it is solely up to the prosecution to move the needle away from innocence and toward guilt, and that it is not the responsibility of the accused person to prove their innocence. Failure to instruct the jury in this way may be grounds for appealing a conviction.

Double Jeopardy

You have the right to have criminal charges against you settled once and for all, and not to have to keep relitigating a crime over and over. To be charged again after you've been either convicted or acquitted is known as double jeopardy, and it's prohibited under the Fifth Amendment.

Help or Hoax?

Plea Bargains

It's estimated that between 90 and 97 percent of all criminal cases are resolved through plea bargaining, rather than going to trial. In a plea bargain, the accused person agrees to plead guilty in exchange for a sentence or punishment that is less harsh than what they might receive after trial. Typically, the charges they plead to are less severe than the original charges.

If you are charged with a crime, you are likely to be offered a plea bargain. You can find a resource at the end of this chapter to help you more fully understand all the implications of a plea bargain. **You'll want to consult an attorney who can help you weigh the pros and cons and make the best possible decision under the circumstances.**

As with many legal matters, though, determining double jeopardy isn't entirely straightforward. If the judge declares a mistrial because the jury couldn't agree on a verdict, you might very well be facing another trial. But if the judge declares a mistrial because, for example, the prosecution intentionally engaged in shady behavior, a retrial might not be allowed. There are other factors to be considered as well, such as how far the prosecution process had gotten before it was interrupted. Generally speaking, though, the government has one chance to prove its case.

Resources to Understand Your Trial Rights

Taylor v. Kentucky, 436 US 478 (1978)

supreme.justia.com/cases/federal/us/436/478

This is the case where the Supreme Court ruled that the jury instructions from the judge must clearly state that the accused is presumed innocent.

Right to Counsel

law.cornell.edu/wex/right_to_counsel

This article gives an overview of the right to effective legal counsel and links to more in-depth articles.

Double Jeopardy

constitution.findlaw.com/amendment5/annotation03.html

Defining double jeopardy can be complicated; this discussion may help your understanding.

Plea Bargain

findlaw.com/criminal/criminal-procedure/plea-bargain.html

You may feel pressured to accept a plea bargain, but you need to carefully consider the implications.

 Involuntary Servitude

Understand Your Labor Rights

Can you be forced to work against your will? Know what the law allows when it comes to prison terms, military service, and general employment.

Sure, the Thirteenth Amendment abolished slavery in the United States back in 1865. But the amendment distinguished between chattel slavery—where one person is considered the property of another—and involuntary servitude, where a person is compelled to work for another but is not owned by them. In fact, it specifically allows involuntary servitude as punishment if you're convicted of a crime.

Prison Labor

 In practical terms, involuntary servitude means if you go to prison you may be forced to work while you're there. In return, you may earn an hourly wage that ranges from about $0.14 to $2.00—or you may be paid nothing at all. Even if you are paid, you are likely to have some portion of your wages withheld to cover the cost of keeping you housed and fed, to pay fines that were part of your sentence, or to pay reparations for your crime.

The traditional argument is that compelling prisoners to work helps in their rehabilitation—they have the opportunity to develop good work habits, and may even learn a trade that will benefit them when they are released. It is also admitted, though, that running a prison takes a lot of manpower, and it would be prohibitively expensive to pay living wages for the necessary work prisoners do.

In 2022 California legislators tried to amend the state's constitution to ban involuntary servitude of prisoners, but the amendment failed. Whereas prisoners in California are currently paid less than $1.00 per hour for their work, it was feared that if the amendment passed they would be able to demand the state's $15.00 per hour minimum wage, which would end up costing taxpayers an estimated $1.5 billion per year.

The penalties for refusing prison work assignments can be harsh. You might lose privileges (including visits from your family) and time earned toward early release; you might even be placed in solitary confinement. Because the Constitution specifically allows involuntary servitude of those convicted of crimes, your options are limited.

Military Conscription

The United States did away with the draft in 1973, converting to an all-volunteer military. However, in 1980 the requirement for all men between the ages of eighteen and twenty-five to register with the Selective Service System was restored. In 2015, gender-based restrictions on military service were lifted, allowing women to serve in

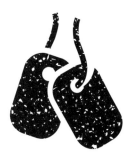

ground combat roles, but so far women have not been required to register for a possible future draft.

Compulsory military service—forcing you to serve against your will—is by definition a form of involuntary servitude. So is it unconstitutional? The Supreme Court has never ruled on whether military conscription in peace time would violate the Thirteenth Amendment, but it has been clear that in times of war, dire national need takes precedence over the amendment's individual protections.

What Happens If You Don't Register?

Men are required to register with the Selective Service within thirty days of turning eighteen. Failure to do so can result in a prison sentence of up to five years and/or a fine of up to $250,000.

How will the government know if you don't register? According to the Selective Service website, they may look for you in the databases of places such as:

★ Department of Motor Vehicles
★ Department of Education
★ Department of Homeland Security
★ Department of Labor's Workforce Innovation and Opportunity Act or Job Corps Program
★ Department of Defense's recruiting
★ Public high schools

DID YOU KNOW?

You can't pre-apply for conscientious objector status; you would only be eligible to apply in the event of a draft.

In the absence of a draft, you probably won't face heavy penalties for failing to register, but you may be ineligible for college financial aid or employment with the federal government.

Conscientious Objection

Even if you would qualify as a conscientious objector in the event of a draft, you are still required to register with the Selective Service. You can't pre-apply for conscientious objector status; you would only be eligible to apply in the event of a draft.

Employment Contracts

If you contract to work for a specified period of time and then quit early, your employer might come after you for monetary compensation, especially if they paid you in advance. They

cannot, however, force you to keep working against your will. Of course, if the financial penalty for not following through on your promise is so heavy that you feel you have no choice and must stay on the job, you might argue you were being forced into involuntary servitude.

Noncompete agreements may in some cases be considered to create a kind of involuntary servitude, especially when they are forced on unskilled, low-wage workers with limited employment prospects. The threat of being unhireable if you quit your current job can be just as binding as physical restraint.

Resource for Understanding Military Registration

Selective Service System

sss.gov

sss.gov/wp-content/uploads/2020/03/MSSA-2003.pdf

Find everything you need to know about the Selective Service. If you are male (according to your birth certificate) and between the ages of eighteen and twenty-five, you are required to register with the Selective Service System.

Jury Duty

Make a Successful Excusal Request

If a jury duty summons has you wanting to run, here's what you need to know about the reality of serving and the accepted reasons you can request excusal.

Should you ever find yourself in court facing criminal charges, you'll want to know the jury is composed of impartial, civic-minded people who will do their best to judge the evidence before them. And should you be summoned for jury duty, your fellow citizens will expect the same of you. The right to a fair trial depends in large part on a properly seated jury.

Depending on the state, prospective jurors may be drawn from voter registration and driver's license records, from local tax rolls, or all three. If you are included in any of these records you may be randomly summoned to appear for jury duty at any time. Whether you look forward to serving on a jury or want to avoid it at all costs, you have rights and options.

Does the Constitution Require Jury Duty?

The US Constitution does not make jury duty mandatory. It does, however, give criminal defendants the right to trial by jury, and that means citizens have to be made available to serve this purpose. If everyone felt jury service was a personal civic obligation to be met whenever possible, there would be no need to compel service. However, not everyone feels this sense of duty, and so each state has laws making jury duty mandatory and setting penalties for refusing to serve.

What If You Don't Respond to a Jury Summons?

A jury summons is issued by the relevant court, and just like any other court summons, responding is not legally an option. When you fail to respond to a jury summons, the court is more interested in compelling your service than punishing you for not serving, so it may go through several steps to get you to show up. In the end, depending on your state's laws, failure to respond may result in a fine of hundreds or thousands of dollars and even your arrest and incarceration.

Can You Legally Get Out of Serving?

Jury duty can last anywhere from hours to several months, depending on the case. This may not be a problem if you have no personal responsibilities, but otherwise being involved in even a short trial may cause you undue hardship. While the law is not on your side if you just ignore a jury summons, there are a number of legitimate reasons to be excused from service. Some generally recognized reasons include:

★ **Financial hardship.** Your employer doesn't have to (and won't) pay you while you're on jury duty and you can't afford not to work. This excuse could also apply if you're a small business owner.

DID YOU KNOW?

While the law is not on your side if you just ignore a jury summons, there are acceptable reasons to be excused from service.

★ **You're needed at home.** You are the sole caregiver for a family member.

★ **Medical reasons.** Maybe you have surgery scheduled or are undergoing treatments you can't miss. (Bring your records as backup.) Pregnancy and breastfeeding could also apply here.

★ **You know someone involved in the case.** You know the accused, or one of the witnesses, or possibly anyone else with a role in the trial.

★ **Full-time student status.** Most states will excuse full-time (and occasionally part-time) students who are attending an accredited college or university.

★ **Age.** In some states, people over a certain age can ask for exemption. Check your state's age requirements for jury service.

★ **Your line of work.** Speak up if you're in an occupation that could influence your view of the case.

To be excused from jury duty, you usually have to show up at the appointed time and explain your reason. If you just want to put off your service until a later date, you can typically do that online or by phone. And keep in mind that reporting for jury duty doesn't mean you'll be selected for a trial—more often than not, you'll be thanked and sent home. In some states, you may be able to check in the night before and find out you don't have to appear at all.

The Difference Between a Grand Jury and a Petit Jury

You may be summoned to serve on either a petit jury or a grand jury. Random selection from public records is the same in either case, but the experiences are entirely different.

What Is a Petit Jury?

A petit, or trial, jury is a six- or twelve-person jury that considers evidence produced by both the prosecution and the defense, and decides whether they believe the defendant is guilty or not. This is the type of jury duty most people get called for.

The jury selection process includes something called "voir dire," in which potential jurors are questioned to determine whether or not they are capable of serving without partiality or bias. By expert estimates, about 80 percent walk away from this stage. As long as you're being truthful, sharing strong opinions at this stage may help you get out of jury duty if that's your goal.

What Is a Grand Jury?

Before the federal government can charge someone with a felony, they have to get an indictment from a grand jury. Some states also seek indictments from grand juries for serious crimes, but not all do.

A grand jury is selected at random from public records, just like a trial jury. Unlike a trial jury, a grand jury:

★ Is composed of up to twenty-three jurors
★ Serves for a specified period of time (up to twelve months) rather than for a specified case
★ Does not go through the voir dire selection process
★ Will see evidence from the prosecution only
★ Will work in secret and be closed to the public
★ Will not have a judge or attorneys present
★ Can submit questions for witnesses

★ Decides by a supermajority of two-thirds or three-fourths of the jurors whether there is enough evidence to indict, or bring charges

A prosecutor may still decide to bring charges even if the grand jury doesn't vote to indict, but they are likely to conclude that if they couldn't convince the grand jury, they wouldn't succeed with a trial jury either.

How Much Does Jury Service Pay?

The compensation for jury duty is highly variable. Depending on the state, daily pay may be as low as $5, and rarely goes above $50. Compensation may or may not include reimbursement for travel expenses—you may even be charged for parking at the courthouse. In some cases, the daily rate increases if your case runs long.

A few states require your employer to continue your regular pay while you are serving on a jury but they are in the minority, and your employer may be able to deduct your jury pay from your wages. And to add insult to the injury of nominal compensation, you must claim your juror pay as taxable income.

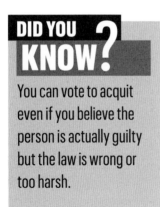

DID YOU KNOW?

You can vote to acquit even if you believe the person is actually guilty but the law is wrong or too harsh.

Jury Nullification

What happens if, as a juror, you believe the defendant is guilty as charged, but don't think they should be punished for their actions? What if you think the law is wrong, or that the consequences are too harsh and out of proportion to the crime?

If you are morally or ethically opposed to conviction, you can vote to acquit even if you believe the person is actually guilty—this is called jury nullification. Because jury verdicts must be unanimous, one juror refusing to convict is enough to deadlock, or hang, the jury and cause a mistrial. If you are the only juror refusing to convict, you may find yourself the object of anger and frustration on the part of your fellow jurors as well as the judge, the lawyers, and anyone else invested in convicting the accused.

On the other hand, some laws actually are unjust, or are applied unfairly or unevenly. Social mores change over time, and laws don't always keep up. Part of the reason Prohibition was repealed was that so many jurors refused to convict people charged with alcohol-related crimes.

Resources for Navigating Jury Duty

Handbook for Trial Jurors Serving in US District Courts
uscourts.gov/sites/default/files/trial-handbook.pdf

Here's everything the government wants you to know about serving on a trial jury.

Handbook for Federal Grand Jurors
uscourts.gov/sites/default/files/grand-handbook.pdf

Here's everything the government wants you to know about serving on a grand jury.

 Legal Tender

Leverage Cash, Community Currency, and Bartering

If you want to detangle yourself from heavy involvement with credit and banks, you have options. Here's what is perfectly legal and what could put you at risk.

Legal tender is anything the government says can be used to fulfill debts and other financial obligations. In the United States, bank notes (paper money) and coins minted by the federal government are the only legal tender recognized by law. When you pay with a check, money order, or credit card, you are basically issuing an IOU that can be exchanged later for legal tender.

 Your creditors are required by law to accept cash—paper money and coins—as payment for debts you've already incurred, but private businesses may be able to refuse to accept cash for new transactions. This is considered unfair to those who don't have debit or credit cards, or bank accounts to back up mobile payment apps, and some states have started passing laws requiring businesses to accept cash.

There was actually a time when private banks could issue their own money, but now only the US Department of the Treasury can print and distribute legal tender here. Centralized control of the country's money supply allows the Fed to balance supply and demand and control monetary policy, attempting to grow the economy while limiting inflation.

DID YOU KNOW?

Some states have started passing laws requiring private businesses to accept cash.

Unless you intend to go entirely off the grid, you will have to depend, at least some of the time, on legal tender to manage your daily finances, no matter how you view the federal government's monopoly on money and its use. That's not to say you have no options at all, though. With alternatives from the ancient (barter) to the new (cryptocurrency), it may be possible to pay bills and obtain goods without resorting to the almighty dollar.

Understanding Commodity Currency Versus Fiat Currency

Any tangible item, from goats to seashells, can be used in exchange for goods and services. Throughout history, though, the most universally valued token of wealth has been gold. While gold is widely accepted as a payment for just about anything, it's not very practical to carry around and if someone steals it, your wealth is gone.

The obvious solution is to keep your gold (or your goats) safely tucked away somewhere secure, and use slips of paper to represent the wealth you have stored. This is known as commodity currency—that is, money that represents a given quantity of a commodity, or tangible item.

US currency was once backed by gold stored in a secure government vault in Fort Knox, Kentucky. The gold standard was tweaked in 1933 and eliminated altogether In 1971, with the United States converting to fiat currency. In this context "fiat" means authorization, and fiat money is backed solely by the good faith and creditworthiness of the government.

How the Dollar's Worth Is Determined

Before 1971, the value of a dollar was tied to a specified amount of gold. Now the value of a dollar is based on factors such as:

★ **Foreign exchange rates,** or how much foreign currency a dollar will buy. The exchange rate fluctuates throughout the day.

★ **Demand for Treasury notes,** issued by the government and guaranteed to pay a set amount of interest after a set amount of time. If demand for Treasury notes is high, the dollar's value rises.

★ **How many dollars other countries are holding** in their central banks. The more value they believe the US dollar has, the more they will keep on hand.

Beware of Fictitious Financial Instruments

You may have heard that because fiat currency is no longer backed by gold or silver, it's worthless or not "real money." It's true that much like the stock market, the value of US currency is based on its perceived worth rather than on anything tangible. However, it's also true that all the major economies of the world rely on fiat money—so if it's a house of cards, it's built with a massive, global deck.

Along these same lines is the belief that you can discharge your personal debts with shrewd use of financial instruments such as bills of exchange and sight drafts that are used legitimately in business contexts (typically involving international trade). The reasoning behind this belief is complex and variable, but the bottom line is that you are not only very unlikely to succeed in settling your debts this way, but you may also be setting yourself up for legal complications with serious consequences.

The Office of the Comptroller of the Currency (OCC), an independent bureau of the Treasury department, advises banks and other financial institutions to refuse to negotiate bills of exchange and similar instruments when they are offered as payment for personal debts. They are advised to retain such an instrument if they receive one, file a suspicious activity report, and submit the instrument and the report to the FBI with copies to the OCC.

Before being seduced by the thought of using this kind of financial sleight of hand to unburden yourself of debt, consider whether you are really prepared for the potential cost of tangling with the Treasury department and FBI in this way. Others who have done so are currently serving lengthy prison sentences.

Can You Pay Your Taxes in Cash?

Perhaps you want to pay your federal taxes but you are "unbanked"—you don't want to (or can't) open a bank account. Can you pay your taxes in cash?

Historically, the IRS has penalized cash payments by adding sizable fees to them, but even that behemoth of a federal agency

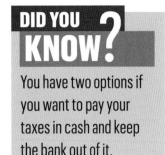
has to keep up with the times. There are some—such as cannabis dispensaries—who are unable to open bank accounts and have no choice but to pay in cash. Now there are two options for paying taxes in cash:

★ **You can pay in person at an IRS taxpayer assistance center** (TAC) that accepts cash. You have to make an appointment and you should call thirty to sixty days before the day you want to pay. (See Resources, at the end of this chapter, for website info.)

★ **You can also pay at a retail partner,** such as Dollar General, Family Dollar, CVS Pharmacy, Walgreens, Pilot Travel Centers, 7-Eleven, and others. There is a small fee per cash payment and there are daily, monthly, and annual limits to the number and amounts of payments you can make. (See Resources for website info.)

Can You Print Your Own Money?

Well, yes . . . and no. You are perfectly free to invent your own currency and use it to trade with anyone willing to accept it. This is the basis of community currency, which is issued by a business or community organization and accepted by participating local businesses. You still have to exchange legal tender for community currency, but you may be able to get it for a discount (that is, pay less than a US dollar for a community dollar). The goal of community currency is to support local businesses and boost the local economy.

There's nothing to stop you from printing your own currency, even if you're not so civic-minded. What you can't do is create a currency that looks like "real" US money, because that's a serious crime. The federal government is not amused by counterfeiting, and the penalties are certain and harsh. You also can't force any unwilling person, business, or governmental entity to accept your personal currency—because it isn't recognized as legal tender, no one has to take it.

What about Copying Money?

It isn't strictly illegal to photocopy money as long as you don't intend to pass it off as legal tender. You might want to use it in a stage play, for example, or in an advertisement. To keep Treasury agents off your doorstep, be sure to make any copies less than 75 percent or more than 150 percent of the size of real dollars, and only copy one side—double-sided photocopies of dollars are prohibited.

How to Get What You Need without Money

Bartering is the exchange of goods or services between people or businesses without the use of money. People engaged in barter transactions long before the invention of currency, and some people still do. If you have a product, skill, or valuable goods to trade, you may be in a position to start bartering for what you want or need.

GOOD FOR YOU!

If you have a product, skill, or valuable goods to trade, you may be in a position to start bartering for what you want or need.

To explore what kind of bartering you might be able to do, you can:

★ Talk to people you know, or negotiate with independent businesses you frequent.
★ Check your city's Craigslist.com listing for a barter section (under "For sale").
★ Search for a local or regional barter exchange, which will allow you to barter for a wide variety of goods and services.

One caveat: The federal government treats goods or services you receive through barter as taxable income, based on the fair market value of whatever you receive. If you provide goods or services to settle business expenses, you *may* be able to deduct some portion. This appears to be limited to the actual out-of-pocket cost of whatever you trade, though; to avoid IRS hassles it would be a good idea to consult with a tax expert before you go that route.

In Case of Emergency, Barter Strategically

If you are inclined to stock up on emergency supplies, you might consider the kinds of nonperishable goods that will be in demand in an emergency—think about how desperate people were for toilet paper at the start of the COVID pandemic! Consider laying in extra supplies of hygiene items, tools, batteries, medical supplies, tobacco, vegetable seeds, and anything else you can think of that your neighbors might need or want in a disaster situation.

Help or Hoax?

Cryptocurrencies

Cryptocurrencies, such as Bitcoin and Ethereum, are virtual currencies that are not issued or controlled by any government. The lack of governmental involvement makes cryptocurrencies appealing to those who want to conduct financial transactions in private. However, the lack of any official backing also makes cryptocurrencies highly unstable, and their lack of standing as legal tender limits how and where you can use them.

Only one country, El Salvador, has attempted to make a cryptocurrency legal tender, and that attempt has been an abject failure. Despite the government offering financial incentives to citizens to use Bitcoin for their transactions, very few do. Even worse, the $100 million the El Salvadoran treasury invested in Bitcoin in 2021 has since lost more than half its value, destroying the country's credit rating and raising the possibility it will default on its debts. It is unlikely the United States will experiment with making cryptocurrencies legal tender any time soon.

Similar to barter, you can exchange cryptocurrencies for goods and services as long as another party is willing to accept them, and you can also sell them outright. The IRS currently considers cryptocurrencies to be property or assets, and any gains you see from selling or exchanging them are subject to taxation, just as with any other capital gains.

Resources for Payment Power

Paying Taxes with Cash

irs.gov/payments/pay-your-taxes-with-cash

pay.vanilladirect.com/pages/retailers

Learn how to avoid penalties for paying your taxes with cash and where you can make payments.

Bartering Basics

investopedia.com/terms/b/barter.asp

Businesses do it, even countries do it; learn how you can do it, too.

IRS Topic No. 420, Bartering Income

irs.gov/taxtopics/tc420

Taxes are inevitable, even when you don't exchange legal tender.

Don't Let Big Tech Steal Your Data

Keep your communications confidential with encryption options and messaging apps known to value privacy. Plus, know your rights when it comes to the data that corporations can collect and the government can access.

Depending on when you got your first cell phone, you may have used SMS (Short Message Service) to send simple text-only messages to your friends and family who also had cell phones. SMS takes text messages from your phone and bounces them from cell tower to cell tower until they reach the desired recipients.

Because SMS uses the same technology as voice calls, it's included as part of the plan offered by your wireless carrier and doesn't require you to have an internet connection. Being able to send messages without an internet connection can be a big plus. Although Wi-Fi is increasingly ubiquitous, there are still times when cell service is all you've got. But there's a big downside to this old-school technology: SMS messages are not secure, and they are not private.

Even using newer technology doesn't always guarantee privacy. The advent of smartphones changed the messaging landscape entirely,

DID YOU KNOW?

SMS messages are not secure, and they are not private.

allowing the introduction of so-called "over-the-top" (OTT) messaging applications that work over the internet, over the top of cellular networks. Popular OTT apps include Facebook Messenger, Apple iMessage, WhatsApp, Skype, and many more. These apps require an internet connection and allow you to send texts, voice messages, photos, videos, and GIFs, and make voice and video calls.

Some OTT messaging apps offer encryption by default, but may do so only for some data—for example, texts but not videos, or vice versa. Other apps may require you to opt in to encryption, leaving you unprotected if you don't know you have to take this step.

The Power of Encryption

In simplest terms, encryption takes the text message (or photo, video, or file) you send from your device and scrambles it into an unreadable form as it travels to your intended recipient, then restores it to its original form when it reaches their device. No one else can read the message while it's in transit, and trying to alter it in any way during its transit will corrupt it so that it becomes permanently unreadable. This is what's known as end-to-end encryption, the kind most commonly used by OTT messaging apps.

SMS messages are not end-to-end encrypted, meaning they can be intercepted and read by anyone with access to them—including your cellular provider, hackers, and law enforcement or others with subpoena powers. The texts themselves are stored on your provider's servers

DID YOU KNOW?

Even after SMS messages are deleted, their metadata is retained.

for variable periods of time, but even after messages are deleted, their metadata is retained. Metadata is data about data. Text message metadata is information gathered about the messages you send, other than the actual content of the messages. It may include who you sent the text to, when you sent it, where you were when you sent it, and possibly more.

Help or Hoax?
No-Cost Messaging Apps

Messaging applications make it easy to keep in touch with friends, family, and coworkers, and the more popular an app is, the more likely someone you want to message is already on it. It's also likely your favorite messaging app is free to use—another bonus, right? But is it really *free*—or are the costs just hidden?

With a few exceptions, messaging apps are designed to make money for someone. But if the app is free to use and doesn't serve you ads—the most obvious way to make money on any platform—where does the money come from?

The popular WhatsApp messaging app, for example, is free to use, doesn't run ads, and has no obvious revenue stream. Yet Facebook (now Meta)—known for its voracious appetite for data—considered it so valuable that in 2014 it paid $19 billion to acquire it.

Why? The ugly truth is that the true value in free-to-use messaging apps lies in their real product: personal information about its users. As made clear in the Netflix documentary *The Social Dilemma*, If you are not paying for the product, *you* are the product. In other words, when you download and use a "free" messaging app that collects your data and tracks your behavior, you are literally paying for the app with your life. Despite the fact that Whatsapp is now owned by Meta, it is end-to-end encrypted, which means that at least messages are secure.

Privacy Policies and Disclosures

In 2020 Apple, maker not just of iPhones and MacBooks but also numerous apps that run on its products, launched privacy labels that have been compared to the nutritional labels found on food products. Apple now requires the information pages for any app downloadable from its app store to list the kinds of data the app tracks or collects.

For example, the WhatsApp privacy label lists the data that "may be collected and linked to your identity" as:

★ Purchases
★ Location
★ Contacts
★ Financial information
★ Contact information
★ User content
★ Usage data
★ Identifiers
★ Diagnostics

To understand what this really means, though, or if you don't get your apps from the Apple app store, you'll need to head over to the WhatsApp website. There, if you take the time to read through the lengthy privacy policy, you'll find the app keeps track of when you use it, how long you use it, what you do when you use it, who you communicate with, and much more.

It also collects information on your phone or computer, including "hardware model, operating system information, battery level, signal strength, app version, browser information, mobile network, connection information (including

GOOD FOR YOU!

If you take the time to read through privacy policies, you'll find what apps keep track of when you use them.

phone number, mobile operator or ISP), language and time zone, IP address, device operations information, and identifiers (including identifiers unique to Meta Company Products associated with the same device or account)."

Additionally, the app both collects information you have about your contacts (phone numbers, names, etc.) and collects from your contacts information they have about you. It also shares your information back and forth with third parties, something over which you have no control.

Can the Government Subpoena Data?

The Fourth Amendment protects you against unreasonable, arbitrary searches and seizures of your personal property. Of course, the amendment's authors were thinking of tangible property—your home, your furnishings, your papers, and so forth. What about intangible property the country's founders couldn't possibly have anticipated—like text messages?

It's important to understand the difference between a search warrant, which is covered under the Fourth Amendment, and a subpoena, which is not. A warrant is issued to someone in law enforcement, and gives them authority to search and seize specific property. A solid showing of probable cause that the sought-after property will reveal evidence of a crime is required to get a warrant.

A subpoena, on the other hand, is a court order to an individual or entity requiring them to give testimony or produce evidence that may be relevant to a civil or criminal proceeding. While it is expected a subpoena will be issued in "good faith," a showing of probable cause is not required.

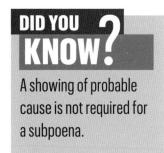
So, while a warrant would be needed before a governmental or law enforcement entity could come into your home and take your phone or laptop, they might only need a subpoena to get your personal information from your cellular or internet service provider.

This is an evolving area of law, and it isn't certain what information, if any, your service provider might be compelled to share. One issue is an exception to Fourth Amendment protection known as the third-party doctrine, which holds that when you reveal personal information to someone else, you relinquish your right to privacy regarding that information. Some courts have held that the data your cellular or internet service provider collects on you is no longer private and can be obtained by subpoena.

How to Protect Your Personal Information

The good news is that there are messaging apps that focus on privacy and empower you to protect your personal data. The bad news is that these apps are not as popular and widely used as the more problematic ones, and to use one you'll need to convince your contacts to make the switch too.

If your friends, family, and coworkers are also worried about the degradation of privacy in the current environment and the monetization of their personal information, they may be willing to make the change in their own best interest. Otherwise, moving them away from what is comfortable and familiar, regardless of the advantages, may be a hard sell.

Of course, it's possible some of your more security-minded contacts have already beat you to it. When you install a new messaging app, you can choose to let it search your contacts to see who else is already onboard. This may feel counterintuitive if you're trying to keep apps from reaching their tentacles into your private life, so you'll have to weigh that against the time and effort it saves you. You'll also have the option of inviting friends to join the app—just give them a heads-up beforehand, so they know the invitation is really coming from you.

Use Disappearing Messages

Many messaging apps offer the option of disappearing messages that self-destruct within a given period of time, anywhere from as soon as they are read by the recipient to many weeks later. This option can usually be turned off and on, and may be applied to some chats and not others.

A disappearing message isn't guaranteed to disappear under all circumstances, of course—the person you send it to can always choose to take a screenshot or photo of the message before it's gone. This feature works best when you trust your chat partner.

Check Your Encryption Settings

Even the most secure messaging apps may require you to opt in to encryption, so you'll need to check an app's settings to make sure you're fully protected.

Resources to Choose a Secure Messaging App

It would be impossible to name every messaging app available to you—as with all technology, failures, successes, and new developments are happening every day. But at the time of publication, the following apps are widely considered the most secure and best for minimizing the amount of data that is, or can be, collected on you.

Signal

signal.org

Signal is unique among messaging apps in that it is owned and developed by an independent 501(c)(3) nonprofit organization. Its funding comes from grants and donations, and it promises it will never be acquired by a for-profit company. The messages you send and calls you make through Signal are encrypted end to end, cannot be viewed or listened in on by Signal or any other third party, and are not stored on Signal servers.

Telegram

telegram.org

Telegram has been developed and financed by Russian brothers Pavel and Nikolai Durov, who now live in Dubai. Telegram offers end-to-end encryption but does save your messages and media on its servers so you can access them from any device. Additionally, the app may retain your metadata for up to twelve months as it seeks to protect its 400+ million users from spam and hackers. Should this worry you? Well, the Durovs spent two years fighting the Russian government's efforts to access users' messages. In the end the Kremlin capitulated, and Telegram has become so popular even Russian government officials use it.

Viber

viber.com/en

Originally developed to allow romantic partners to make internet

(VOIP) phone calls, Viber evolved over time into a full-featured messaging app that was eventually bought by Japanese e-commerce giant Rakuten. Viber offers end-to-end encryption and doesn't store your messages on its servers (except temporarily, until a message reaches its recipient). It also offers a suite of privacy features that allow you to hide your online status, chat without revealing your phone number, delete sent messages even if they've already been read, and more.

Know Your Rights within a Community

You know that if the home you live in is governed by a homeowners association, you will have to live by its rules and regulations. So if you don't have an HOA overseer, you are free to do whatever you like—right? Well, yes . . . and no.

The farther your home is from your neighbors, the more freedom you'll enjoy. Proximity to other homes means your activities can affect others (just as their activities affect you) and that sets up conflict between your rights and theirs. Having neighbors means you may experience—or cause—annoyances and inconveniences that may be either transient or ongoing. How they are handled varies.

What Is a Nuisance?

Legally, a nuisance is anything that unreasonably interferes with the rights of others. It is most commonly applied to the right to peaceful enjoyment of one's own home or property. One neighbor annoying another is committing a private nuisance, while one neighbor annoying the community is committing a public nuisance.

Private Nuisance

Examples of private nuisances include:

- ★ Loud music or noises
- ★ Excessively bright lights
- ★ Smoke
- ★ Noxious fumes
- ★ Storing or working on cars parked in the yard

Obviously, the best way to deal with a private nuisance—something your neighbor is doing that is interfering with your enjoyment of your own property—is to talk to the neighbor and try to work something out. They may not even be aware that what they are doing is causing a problem for you. And the reverse is also true—you may not be aware something you are doing is causing a problem for those around you.

Litigating a Private Nuisance

When a nuisance complaint can't be settled amicably but no law is being broken, the only recourse is litigation. Laws and definitions vary by state, but, generally speaking, in order to win a private nuisance suit against a neighbor, you must prove that:

- ★ You own or have a right to occupy your home or land
- ★ The neighbor has in fact done something that interferes with your right to enjoy your property
- ★ The interference is substantial and unreasonable

Part of proving the last point is showing that the neighbor's behavior wasn't a brief annoyance,

GOOD FOR YOU!

Your best shot at successful litigation will be documenting that the behavior was ongoing, not just one brief annoyance.

such as one loud party, but is ongoing, such as loudly amplified music playing outside every night.

Suing for Trespass

If a neighbor isn't just obnoxious on their own property but physically intrudes on yours, you might be able to sue them for trespass. This is another case where you need to check your local law, but usually to complain of trespass you must show that you advised the other person they were trespassing and they refused to leave or stop what they were doing anyway.

Attractive Nuisance

Nuisances that put children in danger fall into a category of their own, known as attractive nuisances. An attractive nuisance is one

that is likely to appeal to a small child, but then poses a threat to their safety if they come near. The most common attractive nuisances in residential areas are swimming pools. Others examples include, but are not limited to:

★ Trampolines
★ Tree houses
★ Wells
★ Tunnels
★ Ladders

If you have an attractive nuisance on your property, you are obligated to do everything you can to keep children away from it, including fencing it in, locking it up, or otherwise making it as difficult as possible for a child to access it. It might seem reasonable to expect parents to supervise their children and keep them away from your property, but you're the one who will be held liable if a child gets hurt.

Public Nuisance

A public nuisance is one that affects not just the nearest neighbor but also the community at large. Whereas the recourse for a private nuisance is civil litigation, public nuisances may result in criminal charges because they pose a threat to the health, safety, comfort, morals, or convenience of the community. A few examples include:

★ Polluting or blocking a public waterway
★ Dealing illegal drugs
★ Storing or using explosives, including illegal fireworks
★ Keeping an animal known to be vicious

Because public nuisances generally involve criminal behavior, they are dealt with by government and law enforcement agencies. If you're the offending party, you'll want to arrange for legal representation.

Should You Call the Police?

Some activities don't rise to the standard of nuisance, but do interfere with the right of others to enjoy their home or property, at least temporarily. These are generally activities that, while distressing, are shorter in nature than nuisances.

Criminal Behavior

If a neighbor is committing a crime, rather than just being annoying, you'll have to decide whether what they're doing is serious enough to involve law enforcement. Depending on the neighbor, the neighborhood, and the culture and quality of the local police department, doing so may either fix the problem or make it much worse. You'll have to weigh your own safety—if you're in immediate danger, you really have no choice. But if letting it go this time emboldens the offender to escalate their criminal activity, that could end up being even more dangerous.

Violating Local Ordinances

Many municipalities have rules and regulations that cover annoying behavior. Many communities, for example, have "quiet hours" ordinances that prohibit loud noises, including amplified music and lawn mowers, during certain hours of the day or night. Other issues commonly addressed by local ordinances include:

- ★ Dogs barking
- ★ Number and type of animals kept, and whether inside or outside
- ★ Lawn maintenance

Enforcement of these kinds of ordinances generally falls to the relevant local agency. Animal complaints, for example, are likely handled by animal control. Your city or county likely has a website that lists all the municipal offices and which one to contact for various complaints.

Resources for Neighbor Relations

Overview of Nuisance Law

apha.org/-/media/Files/PDF/factsheets/
Overview_of_Nuisance_Law_factsheet.ashx

Here's a quick read that covers the basics.

Attractive Nuisances

findlaw.com/realestate/owning-a-home/dangers-to-children-attractive-nuisances.html

Protect your neighborhood children from danger, and protect yourself from liability.

When to Call the Cops on a Neighbor

nolo.com/legal-encyclopedia/when-call-the-cops-neighbor.html

You probably hope the answer is never.

Reduce Your Reliance on Public Utilities

Living off the grid is the ultimate in freedom and independence, and doesn't have to mean giving up all the conveniences of modern life. Discover all the ways you can support yourself.

It may be possible to go off the grid on most utilities even in an urban or suburban location, but for total self-sufficiency you'll want land that is remote enough to avoid local restrictions, regulations, and codes. The more your activity affects the convenience, safety, or livelihood of others, the more limited your options will be. Here's where to seek your freedom.

Water

Having a source of water is critical to your ability to live off the grid. There are three basic sources of water: air (rainwater harvesting, atmospheric water harvesting/generation), surface (rivers, streams, lakes, ponds), and ground (wells, springs). You will have at least one source available to you no matter where you are located, but the setup cost, practicality, and legal ramifications will vary.

Rainwater Harvesting

Harvesting, or collecting, rainwater is legal in all fifty states. Some states actively encourage rainwater harvesting to relieve pressure on stormwater drainage systems and preserve other water sources. Some states, though, have regulations that tightly restrict the practice to make sure local aquifers aren't depleted.

The simplest rainwater harvesting system is a barrel that collects gutter runoff. Water harvested this way is suitable for watering gardens and perhaps filling your toilet, but not for drinking. If you want potable rainwater, you'll need to invest in a filtering and purification system.

Atmospheric Water Harvesting

If you've ever run a dehumidifier, you've pulled water from the air in a process known as atmospheric water harvesting. You may have dumped or drained the water the dehumidifier collected, but you could have used it to water your garden instead. In fact, if you filtered and purified the water you could probably have drunk it.

Even very dry areas have a large amount of water stored in the air above them, and atmospheric water harvesting can be feasible almost anywhere. A number of options are available if you have electricity to run them; otherwise, there are harvesting devices that are solar powered (see Resources at the end of this chapter).

Surface Water Sources

Water rights laws vary by region, state, and body of water and can be complex.

Navigable Versus Non-Navigable

When it comes to deciding who has rights to a body of water, the first consideration with a lake or river is whether or not it is navigable. Traditionally, a navigable body of water has been one that a commercial vessel could traverse while plying a trade. In some cases now, navigability also applies to the use of recreational vessels.

Generally speaking, navigable bodies of water belong to the state in which they are located, and are open to public use. Owning property on or around a navigable body of water doesn't give you a private interest in that water.

Lakes and Ponds

If you have a non-navigable lake or pond that is entirely on your land, you can freely draw on it for irrigation or other uses. Still water like this requires even more careful filtration and purification to make it potable, though. And if your lake or pond is replenished solely by rainwater, rather than from a river or stream, there are limits to how much water you can safely pull without making it unviable.

If you own land that borders a lake, you will likely have the right to enter the water, but may need a permit to divert any water from it. Laws vary from state to state.

DID YOU KNOW?

Your rights to water running through your land depend in part on whether or not it is navigable.

Rivers and Streams

As with lakes and ponds, your rights to a river running through your land depend in part on whether or not it is navigable. If it is, it's considered public property and you may or may not have the right to draw reasonable amounts of water from it. You may have similar rights to a non-navigable stream; if it flows through your land

and continues on through land that is not yours, you may have the right to draw reasonable amounts of water as long as you don't affect anyone downstream from you.

Groundwater: Springs and Wells

Water stored in an underground aquifer may be accessed either from a natural spring that brings water to the surface or from a well drilled down into the aquifer. You usually have the right to the groundwater under your property, but this will vary by location. Whether and how much you can pull may depend on whether the aquifer is readily replenished and on how your water use affects others who rely on the same source.

If the source of your groundwater is actually an underground river or stream, your state may designate water rights the same as it does for surface rivers and streams.

Electricity

Home electricity didn't become common in the United States until the 1930s, and then it was mostly limited to urban areas—it would be decades before it became common in more rural areas. You can certainly choose to do without electricity altogether, but there are also ways for you to draw on the natural world to generate your own power.

Solar Energy

Solar panels on home roofs are becoming an increasingly common sight in urban, suburban, and rural areas. You can choose to keep all the solar power you generate for your own use, but if you don't mind being connected to a local power company, you may be able to actually sell them any excess electricity you generate. If you do want to remain entirely off the grid, you'll need a battery system to store electricity for times when the sun is not shining.

Wind Energy

If your land is in a spot where winds blow in a consistent direction rather than tumbling about in variable directions, you may be able to fulfill your power needs with a wind turbine. As with solar power, you can run your turbine either entirely off the grid or connected to a power company that will either buy your excess or credit you what you generate. Depending on your location, it may make sense to have a hybrid solar and wind system that makes the most of your seasonal conditions.

Microhydropower Energy

If your land has a source of running water, a microhydropower system can provide a steady source of power that doesn't rely on weather conditions that vary from day to day, although there may still be seasonal variations in a river or stream's flow. These systems are powered by turbines that rest in the stream or river and are turned by the water's movement. Turbines have been developed that can generate electricity from as little as thirteen inches of moving water.

Sewer

Living off the grid means saying goodbye to the convenience of flushing away biological waste and never thinking about it again. You'll need a way to deal with waste that is sanitary and doesn't foul your local water systems.

One option is to install a septic tank. This is a large metal or concrete tank buried underground. Sewage from your home flows into the tank, where solid waste naturally separates from wastewater. The water portion is deposited even deeper underground, where it filters through soil and back into the groundwater. The solid waste will need to be removed from time to time.

Another option is using a waterless composting toilet. There are several different kinds, but usually they are designed to separate urine from feces. The urine, which is normally sterile, can be allowed to filter through soil like water from a septic tank, or used as fertilizer due to its naturally high nitrogen content. Feces is composted, sometimes with the help of earthworms. Because composting won't kill all the potentially pathogenic microbes in feces, it isn't recommended to use composted solid waste on food crops.

Internet

Other than driving to the nearest town to cadge Wi-Fi from a library or coffee shop, there's no way to get free internet access off the grid. If you want to be able to get online in a rural area, you'll need some kind of gear and at least a basic access plan. Currently there are three options:

★ **Satellite internet.** Depending on your location, you may find satellite service to be unbearably slow, but this should improve as technology advances and more satellites are put into service.

★ **Mobile phone data plan.** Cell coverage is increasingly ubiquitous even in fairly remote areas. You can access the internet directly on your phone or use it as a hotspot for your tablet or laptop.

★ **Portable Wi-Fi hotspot.** These devices work like your cell phone but offer faster downloads, longer battery life, and the ability to connect multiple devices. You'll still have to buy a data plan.

Communications

You have options for communicating locally and even around the world off the grid, without paying for service.

Amateur (Ham) Radio

Operating an amateur, or ham, radio station does require you to get a license from the Federal Communications Commission (FCC), but once you do you'll be able to send and receive radio transmissions far and wide.

Walkie-Talkie

Walkie-talkies are kind of like handheld ham radios. They generally operate on two frequencies, Family Radio Service (FRS) and General Mobile Radio Service (GMRS). FRS is low powered and has very limited range, whereas GMRS is more powerful and has wider range. The FCC requires a license for GMRS use because it could interfere with other radio transmissions, but it's common knowledge that this requirement is rarely if ever enforced.

Satellite Phone

Instead of bouncing signals off cell towers, satellite phones bounce signals off satellites orbiting the Earth, extending their range far beyond what cell phones can offer. You still have to pay to place calls to and from a satellite phone, though, and it will cost you considerably more than cell phone service.

Resources to Find Freedom Off the Grid

Water Law

nationalaglawcenter.org/overview/water-law

Start here for information about legal issues with water use.

Rainwater Harvesting Laws

worldwaterreserve.com/is-it-illegal-to-collect-rainwater

Laws may change over time, but this list of state rainwater harvesting laws has been recently updated and provides lots of useful links for each state.

Solar-Powered Atmospheric Water Generation

source.co

Learn about technology that allows you to collect water from the air without a separate source of electricity.

Solar Panel Planning

bobvila.com/articles/how-many-solar-panels-to-power-a-house

Do the math to see how much of an investment it will take to run your home on solar power.

Wind Electric Systems

energy.gov/energysaver/installing-and-maintaining-small-wind-electric-system

Learn about home wind power systems running both on and off the grid.

Microhydropower Systems

energy.gov/energysaver/microhydropower-systems

Start here to get an idea of how you can generate power from running water.

Amateur Radio Service

fcc.gov/wireless/bureau-divisions/mobility-division/amateur-radio-service

You'll need a license from the FCC to operate a ham radio.

Defend Your Child's Best Interests

You and your child's school may agree that you want the best outcomes for your child, but conflict arises when you disagree on how to get there. Know the rights you have in the educational process.

The rights of parents to make decisions about their children's education has become an increasingly hot topic, but parents have always had concerns about what happens in the government schools their children are bound by law to attend. Private schools and homeschooling offer parents more control but are not practical for every family. Your child doesn't have to leave all their rights at the schoolhouse door, though, and neither do you.

Standardized Tests

Standardized tests are exactly what they sound like: These are tests in which every student in the same grade is asked the exact same questions on the exact same topics, which must be answered in an objective, uniform way—either by multiple choice, or by choosing true or false. This allows direct comparison of academic achievement between children in the same class, the same school, the same district, and state- and nationwide.

DID YOU KNOW?

Evidence suggests standardized tests often fail to reach their goals and, some argue, actually harm the children they are meant to help.

The stated goals of standardized testing are admirable, but evidence suggests tests often fail to reach those goals and, some argue, actually harm the children they are meant to help.

Why Give Standardized Tests?

Standardized tests are meant to provide useful insight into how well students are learning the topics being taught, and to identify areas where they need more support. The idea is that gathering this information can not only help individual students who may be falling behind, but also to figure out what kind of changes need to be made in schools where large numbers of students are failing to meet academic targets, especially in reading and math. The aim is to work toward educational equity—to provide at-risk students with the resources they need to make sure they have the same opportunities in life as those in more affluent schools.

Currently, federal law requires all students in public schools to be given standardized math and reading tests every year in grades 3 through 8, and once in high school. Some schools may give tests more than once per year.

A Brief History of Federal Involvement in Standardized Testing

The Elementary and Secondary Education Act (ESEA) of 1965, part of the Johnson administration's "war on poverty," was intended to direct federal funding to low-performing schools in distressed areas of the country.

It was followed by the No Child Left Behind Act (NCLB) of 2001, which set the unrealistic goal of bringing every student in every school up to grade level by 2014. Schools that couldn't meet the set targets were penalized by having funding withheld.

In 2015, NCLB became the Every Student Succeeds Act (ESSA), which gives schools more options in assessing student progress and designing programs to improve performance. ESSA recognizes every degree of improvement and removes punitive measures for schools that struggle.

ESSA provides federal funds to the states, each of which figures out how to distribute the money equitably. Some way is needed to gather information on which students and which schools need the most help and what kind of help is needed, and to see what works and how much progress is being made. So far, no one has come up with a more effective way to make this assessment than by using standardized tests.

What's the Downside to Standardized Testing?

There are several objections to the use of standardized tests. Among them are:

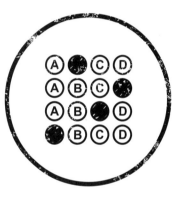

- ★ Too much time is devoted to "teaching to the test," prioritizing test preparation over education
- ★ Inherent bias in standardized tests makes it inevitable that certain students will underperform
- ★ Poor test results may be used to target certain schools for closure

Can You Opt Out of Standardized Tests?

ESSA requires schools to test 95 percent of their students each year that tests are required, and administrators do their best to achieve that goal. However, some parents choose to opt their children out of standardized testing, and some educators support that choice. Currently, some states fully allow opting out, some allow it with conditions, and some outlaw it altogether.

Permitted Opting Out

A few states allow parents to opt their children out of all standardized testing without individual penalties. They do warn, however, that if their school district fails to meet the requirement to test 95 percent of eligible students, it could lose federal funding. So far, this doesn't seem to have happened.

Opting Out with Conditions

Some states allow students to refuse to sit for tests, but don't allow blanket opting out. Some allow refusal of some tests but not others, and they may set criteria for test refusal, such as having a stated religious or medical reason.

Opting Out Not Permitted

Most states do not allow opting out of standardized testing. Obviously, they can't actually force a child to sit in a seat and perform, but they may tie test taking to attendance, grades, and even graduation.

How to Opt Out

If your state permits opting out, it probably has a form it would like you to fill out and submit to the school before testing is scheduled to begin. You'll be expected to submit the form each year that you want to opt out.

DID YOU KNOW?

In some states, opting out of standardized tests is considered an act of civil disobedience.

If your state does not permit opting out, you should write a letter to the principal of your child's school. Give your child's name, the standardized test(s) you do not want them to take during the current or upcoming school year, and state that you would like the school to provide some appropriate educational activity during the time the test is being administered.

You may receive pushback from the school on your choice to opt your child out of testing, ranging from gentle persuasion to strong-arm efforts. The National Education Association warns that in some states, opting out is an act of civil disobedience. See Resources, at the end of this chapter, for a link to the NEA's advice on how to advocate for opting out.

Curricula and Educational Materials

An educated citizenry is considered to be essential to democracy. Ideally, children will gain enough competency in math, English, science, and other academic subjects to fully participate in civil life and be productive members of society. Efforts have been made to establish nationwide educational standards, while leaving each state and individual school district free to choose curricula and educational materials that best meet the needs of their local populace.

The different layers of state and local decision makers—from legislators and school board members to school principals and teachers—are filled with people of widely varying educational backgrounds, training, and personal philosophies, which sometimes creates conflict over what and how children in public schools should be taught. The increasing involvement of parents in making these decisions has only added to the difficulty in reaching consensus.

How much say you have in the textbooks and other materials used in your child's classroom, and the books carried in their school library, varies according to your school district's practices. Some districts make all books and materials readily available for parents to review, either online or in person. In some cases you may be able to opt out of specific textbooks, lesson plans, or library books for your child.

See Resources, at the end of this chapter, for information on identifying and contacting your local school district. Following the link to the district's website will allow you to find out more about individual schools, instructional resources, services offered, school board meetings, and opportunities for volunteering.

Homeschooling

Homeschooling offers you the ultimate in parental oversight and control of your child's education. Some states in the not-too-distant past took a punitive approach to homeschooling, threatening to jail parents or take away their children if they kept them at home. Currently, however, homeschooling is legal in all fifty states.

The closure of schools during the COVID pandemic normalized at-home instruction and gave many families who had never considered homeschooling a taste of what it could be like. Not all states have tallied the numbers, but those that have report that homeschooling boomed during lockdown. Although not all families stuck with it when schools reopened, there are far more children being homeschooled now than before schools closed.

The level of governmental intrusion into homeschooling practices varies widely by state. The Home School Legal Defense Association (see Resources) characterizes state laws as:

★ **No notice, low regulation:** No notification from parents to their local school district or any other governmental agency is required.

★ **Low regulation:** Parents are required to notify their local school district.

★ **Moderate regulation:** Parents must send a notification, test scores, and/or professional evaluation of student progress to their local school district.

GOOD FOR YOU!

Homeschooling is now a legal option in all fifty states.

★ **High regulation:** Parents must send notification and achievement test scores and/or professional evaluation, plus other requirements (i.e., curriculum approval by the state, teacher qualification of parents, or home visits by officials).

What If You Don't Comply with Homeschooling Laws?

Every state, even if it has low homeschooling regulation, has compulsory school age laws. A typical age range for compulsory schooling is six or seven years to about sixteen years, although this varies.

Homeschooling laws are intended to ensure a child who is not physically attending school is still receiving an adequate education. Failing to comply with your state's homeschooling laws on notification, testing, and so forth can result in your child being labeled a truant. And depending on how vigorously your district prosecutes truancy, penalties for both you and your child may be severe.

Truancy

Whether your child is being homeschooled or attends a private or public school, they are subject to state compulsory schooling laws. In addition to being enrolled in school (whether at home or elsewhere), the law limits the number of days a child may be absent from school before they are considered to be truant.

Penalties for the Truant Child

Depending on your state's laws, your truant child may be:

★ Given poor grades
★ Prevented from participating in sports or other activities

★ Referred to juvenile court
★ Placed in foster care
★ Sent to juvenile detention

Penalties for the Truant Child's Parents

Parents are responsible for their minor child's welfare, and it is far more common for parents to be penalized for a child's truancy than for the child to be punished. Parents whose child is found to be truant may be required to:

★ Pay fines
★ Perform community service
★ Attend parenting classes
★ Serve jail time for unpaid fines

Help or Hoax?
School Refusal Disorder

There's no psychiatric diagnosis for a child who won't go to school, but there is a recognized disorder known as school refusal. It is assumed there is an underlying reason for a child refusing to go to school, whether it's anxiety, depression, fear of bullying, or some other problem.

If you want your child to go to school but they won't go, the school itself may be able to help. See if there is a counselor or other trained staff who can help identify the cause of your child's reluctance. At the very least, they should be able to refer you to someone outside the school who can help.

Solving the problem of school refusal may be simple or very complicated, depending on what's going on with your child. Either way, dealing with the problem proactively can help your child avoid the truancy label and related penalties.

Resources for Choice in Education

The National Center for Fair and Open Testing

fairtest.org

Visit this website for information on testing at all grade levels, and how to go about opting out.

Opt-Out Policies by State

nasbe.org/opt-out-policies-by-state

State laws can change at any time, but this resource is a good place to start.

Search for Public School Districts

nces.ed.gov/ccd/districtsearch

Start here for information on your local school district and your child's school, and how you can take part in setting educational standards.

Homeschool Laws by State

hslda.org/legal

Get all the details needed to comply with your state's homeschooling laws.

Recording Devices

Keep Recordings from Crossing the Line

From video surveillance in stores and at our doors to social stars looking for the next viral post, we live life on camera. But when does capturing the moment as audio, video, or photo become an invasion of privacy?

According to nonpartisan fact tank Pew Research Center, at least 85 percent of Americans own a smartphone, which can be used to capture and share photographic and video images at the touch of a button. With a US population of over 330 million and growing, that's more than 280 million pocket-size recording devices moving about the country. Add in the growing numbers of doorbell cameras, recreational drones, and camera glasses, and that's a potent mix of potential citizen surveillance.

DID YOU KNOW?

There are more than 280 million pocket-size recording devices moving about the country.

If you prioritize your personal privacy, you may wonder what your rights are when others around you pull out their devices and start recording. And beyond basic privacy concerns, you may be concerned with the possibility they could share their recordings with local or federal law enforcement.

On the other hand, you may have safety and security concerns that make doorbell cameras and other recording devices pretty appealing. What happens when your right to monitor your own porch and yard runs up against the privacy rights of those on the sidewalk, street, or nearby property who happen to be captured on your cameras?

What Is "Reasonable Expectation of Privacy"?

When there's a conflict between the right of one person to record what's happening around them and the right of another person to avoid being recorded, the fundamental issue is whether the latter has a "reasonable expectation of privacy," also known as the "right to be left alone." Generally speaking, you enjoy a reasonable expectation of privacy in your home, but when you venture out in public you forfeit that expectation. There are certain exceptions and, as usual, those exceptions vary from state to state.

For example, you have a reasonable expectation of privacy in a public restroom, or in your gym's locker room. Doctor's offices and AA meetings also apply here. And you probably have some expectation of privacy in your car, although the law on that is far from settled.

Someone doesn't have to physically invade your private property in order to violate your right to privacy. Using a telephoto lens to zoom into your home from across the street would also be a violation. And in many states, flying a camera-equipped drone over your backyard may also be illegal.

Audio Recording Is Different

The law treats recording your voice differently from recording your image. Federal law requires one-party consent to recordings of

phone calls and conversations, meaning at least one of the people taking part in the conversation or call must know it's being recorded and consent to the recording. (Exceptions are obviously made for law enforcement purposes.) Some states require all-party consent, meaning everyone participating in the call or conversation must consent to recording.

The expectation of privacy in conversation underlies restrictions on this kind of recording. But what about recording video in a public place when that video also includes audio? This is another area where the law is evolving, unsettled, and likely to vary from one jurisdiction to another.

Questions come up when, for example, a state transit authority wants to add audio to video surveillance cameras on public buses. On the one hand, a bus is a public space without an expectation of privacy, and audio recordings may enhance everyone's safety. On the other hand, there's a good argument that you retain the right to have private conversations even when you are out in public.

Can Someone Share Your Image?

Say someone has recorded your image in a public place where you had no reasonable expectation of privacy—on the street, on the beach, at a protest rally. What if they want to share your image with others, say in a newspaper, or on social media?

By law, when you take a photograph or video, you own the copyright on that photograph or video, and how it's used is up to you. When it comes to images of other people, there are some exceptions.

The Right of Publicity

In a nutshell, you have the right to control who makes money off your image. You have little recourse if someone records you, without your consent, in a place where you have no reasonable expectation of privacy— but if they make money from the recording, they violate your right of publicity.

The maker of your favorite recreational beverage, for example, can't snap a photo of you, can in hand, and use it in an ad without your permission. Likewise, while the average citizen may be able to record and share your coffee shop meltdown without repercussions, someone who earns a living making this specific kind of embarrassing TikTok videos probably can't.

Intentional Infliction of Emotional Distress

If someone who just happens to be present records a video of you behaving badly in public and shares it online, causing you to lose your job . . . well, that's on you. But if they intentionally provoked you to behave in a way you otherwise would not have done just for the purpose of humiliating you and causing you to suffer personal losses, that's different—that could be considered intentional infliction of emotional distress.

Copyright Violations

You may have seen news stories about police who blast copyrighted music from their cars when people are trying to record their actions. They do this because while they can't stop you from recording them in a public space, if you try to share your video online your social media platform will filter out your video due to copyright violation.

Police departments have made it clear this is not departmental policy and not something officers should ever do. Aside from the optics of police using sneaky tactics to avoid accountability, it may be argued that by broadcasting the music to the public, the police officers are themselves violating copyright law. There is also a good argument that the music is incidental background noise that you could not avoid while exercising your First Amendment right to record the police action, rather than an intentional copyright violation.

How to Protect Your Privacy When Recording Is Ubiquitous

Protecting your privacy in places where you have a reasonable expectation of that privacy is a matter of vigilance—knowing who might try to record you, how they might try, and how to thwart their efforts. Protecting yourself in public spaces is trickier—the best you can do is be aware of what others are doing and try to avoid getting caught up in their surveillance.

Protecting Your Privacy at Home

You may not worry about secret spy cameras in your own home, but you may not have the same level of comfort when it comes to a hotel room or Airbnb. You have a reasonable expectation of privacy in these temporary homes, too, but less control over the actions of others.

Scan for Hidden Cameras

There are a number of ways to check for hidden cameras, which can be very small and discreet and embedded in just about anything. If you have serious security concerns, you might invest in a radio frequency (RF) detector or similar gadget, but there are some easy low-tech detection methods that need nothing more than your senses and your phone.

★ At night or with the curtains drawn, turn out the lights and slowly scan the room for tiny red lights, which many hidden devices will have on when active. Some lights might be more visible if you view them through your phone's camera.

★ While the room is dark, use a flashlight or camera flash to look for glints of light reflecting off a camera lens.

★ Look for wires or power cords that don't seem to belong to a lamp, TV, or other typical appliance.

★ Make a call on your cell phone and slowly walk around the room. Listen closely for crackling sounds, which could be caused by interference from a hidden electronic device.

Check the Devices on Your Network

Wireless cameras and listening devices may connect to and transmit over your Wi-Fi. You can download a free mobile app such as Fing that will scan your Wi-Fi network for connected devices. Check the list for the devices you recognize, and look for any that seem suspicious or out of place.

Look Out for Drones

The issue of whether drone operators have the right to fly over private property is fraught. Federal, state, and local laws have taken different approaches to how much of the airspace over your property is under your control. One thing that is pretty well established is that while a drone that hovers over you while you are sunbathing in your backyard may be invading your

privacy and creating a nuisance, if you try to shoot it down you are likely to face far stiffer penalties than the offending drone operator.

If you are having a problem with a nuisance drone, first try to reason with its owner, if you know who they are. Otherwise, you can file a police report. All but the very smallest drones in the United States now have to be registered with the Federal Aviation Administration (FAA) and so it may be possible to track an offending drone to its owner.

Guard Your Privacy in Public

Other than avoiding public spaces altogether, your only real defense against being recorded by your fellow citizens is to be aware of who might be pointing a recording device in your direction. If you think someone is capturing your image, the safest reaction is to turn away or move away. If you're not averse to confrontation, you can always ask them to stop, but keep in mind that even this simple action can escalate in ways you don't anticipate.

Be Mindful of Implied Consent

Laws about surveillance are constantly changing, but the concept of implied consent is likely to hold in any case. Basically, if you enter or remain in a place after you've been notified recording is taking place, you are presumed to have consented to being recorded. If a store or bank posts a sign at the entrance saying video cameras are in use, you've been notified even if you don't bother to read the sign. A sign may not even be required if the cameras are placed so their presence is obvious.

Be Aware of Camera Glasses

Ray-Ban, as one big-name example, has partnered with Facebook/ Meta to design sunglasses that record pictures and videos that can later be uploaded to Facebook. A sure giveaway of any kind of smart glasses is seeing the wearer using the touch controls in the temples, or sides of the glasses, but Ray-Ban Stories also allow voice commands.

To clue in bypassers, the glasses have a bright white light that flashes when a photo is taken and stays on continuously when video is being recorded. Of course, it wouldn't be hard to cover up the light on the black frames with a bit of electrical tape, so your best bet is still to be sensitive to suspicious behavior.

What Rights Do You Have to Record Others?

If you want to be the one recording other people, whether in private or in public, there are some things you need to keep in mind.

Recording in Private

You may make audio, photographic, and video recordings of other people in the privacy of your own home, as long as you have their consent. The obvious presence of active recording devices may suffice for implied consent.

Recording in Public

You may take photos and videos of others in public places where they have no expectation of privacy, being mindful that they retain their right to privacy in areas such as restrooms, locker rooms, and dressing rooms. You may not make audio recordings of their private conversations, and probably cannot record videos that include audio of private conversations.

You Can't Necessarily Record Everywhere

If a business or an individual tells you not to record on their private property, you must respect their wishes. If you keep recording and don't leave when they tell you to, you can be arrested for trespassing. Courts have ruled that the government has, at least in some cases, the right to prohibit recording in its buildings (for instance, courthouses) even though technically they are public spaces.

Recording the Police

Law enforcement officers may not like being recorded, but in addition to having no expectation of privacy in public spaces they are public servants, and the public has a right to observe them in action. If you don't comply when they tell you to step back, though, you risk being arrested for interfering with their duties.

Even if you are arrested or otherwise harassed when recording the police, they cannot legally take your device, film, or media storage card from you—that would require a court order. In fact, no one is allowed to take your camera away from you in a public place. Even if you're trespassing, the property owner cannot confiscate your camera (or film or SD card) without a court order.

Sharing Your Recordings

You own the copyright to your recordings and generally may share them as you wish, keeping in mind the caveats about right of publicity, intentional infliction of emotional distress, and including copyrighted material in your recordings.

Resources for Understanding Recording Rights

Drone Laws by State

findlaw.com/consumer/consumer-transactions/drone-laws-by-state.html

Whether you operate a drone or have other people's drones buzzing around you, it's good to know your, and their, rights.

Recording Phone Calls and Conversations, by State

justia.com/50-state-surveys/recording-phone-calls-and-conversations

Check whether your state requires one-party consent or all-party consent to recording personal conversations.

Taking Photos and Making Recordings

aclupa.org/en/know-your-rights/know-your-rights-when-taking-photos-and-making-video-and-audio-recordings

This article from the American Civil Liberties Union (ACLU) covers your right to record in public places, with an emphasis on recording police activity.

Understand What the First Amendment Means for You

Whether you follow one faith, are open to many, or reject them all, the First Amendment enshrines your freedom of choice. Here are some areas where faith matters meet public sector and how courts have ruled.

America's founders were not all of the same faith, but in writing and passing the First Amendment they agreed that religious belief was an individual matter, and that the government should stay out of it. They made it clear that religion and government were each best protected by remaining independent of the other.

According to the First Amendment, the United States, unlike England, is never to promote or support any religion, or to establish a state religion—this is the part of the amendment known as the

Establishment Clause. At the same time, the amendment's Free Exercise Clause gives you, as an American citizen, the right to follow any religion or no religion at all.

Thomas Jefferson coined the term "separation of church and state" in 1802,

reinforcing the principle that while most Americans profess religious faith of some kind, the country's government is and should remain secular. There are those who believe otherwise, of course, and tension between the two viewpoints is ongoing.

Blue Laws

In Colonial times, "blue laws" (nobody really knows where the name came from) prohibited a wide variety of activities—from hunting to dancing—on Sunday, the Christian Sabbath. Over time, such laws came to focus more on preventing the sale of alcohol and keeping retail stores closed on Sundays. Today, many states have done away with blue laws altogether, but others still have restrictions on sales of alcohol, motor vehicles, and sex toys, while others regulate hunting and other sports.

Blue laws would seem to be a violation of the Establishment Clause, as they were originally based on religious practices. However, in 1961 the Supreme Court ruled that a day of rest was good for everyone regardless of religious affiliation (or lack thereof), and states should be able to limit Sunday activities if they wanted to (see Resources, at the end of this chapter, for laws by state).

Religion and Schools

Private religious schools are obviously free to promote prayer and religious expression—that's very central to their mission. Public schools, on the other hand, are government institutions and are subject to the Establishment Clause. Historically, it's been clear that while students are free to hold and express their religious faith while attending public schools, religious activity could not be part of the school day.

Recent Court Rulings

In 2022, the Supreme Court ruled on two cases concerning religion in the public sphere—specifically, schools. In these cases, the court overrode decades of judicial precedent.

In *Carson v. Makin*, the court ruled that the state of Maine, which has a program that pays private school tuition for students who don't have a local public school, must include religious schools in its tuition program.

In *Kennedy v. Bremerton School District*, the court ruled in favor of a public high school football coach who left his job after he was told to stop holding post-game prayers on the football field. Rather than praying privately, which has always been allowed, the coach prayed on the fifty-yard line, surrounded by players from his and opposing teams. Although courts have ruled repeatedly that public school employees may not lead students in prayer on school property during school-related activities, in this case the court ruled that the Free Exercise Clause took precedence over the Establishment Clause, and that the coach's prayer should have been allowed.

Religious and Parochial Schools

Schools that are founded on the basis of a particular religion may be considered either a private religious school, which is financed by tuition and fundraising, or a parochial school, which charges tuition but is also funded by a particular church.

Some religious and parochial schools only accept students of a particular faith, but many welcome students of any (or no) faith. You may choose a religious or parochial school for your child not because you are of its faith but because it offers superior academic instruction, but keep in mind these schools will still require religious education and participation in religious activities for all students.

Prayer in Schools

Your child is free to pray in school. What is not allowed is for staff to lead students in prayer during the school day, in time meant for academic instruction. Extracurricular clubs that meet outside of the regular school day are free to engage in prayer and expression of religious beliefs.

If your child attends a public school, they cannot be pressured into praying or taking part in any kind of religious activity. As mentioned, if they attend a private religious or parochial school, they may be required to at least go through the motions of praying.

Religion and Employment Law

According to the US Equal Employment Opportunity Commission (EEOC), your employer may not treat you differently either because you follow a particular religion or because you don't. You can't be harassed for your religious, moral, or ethical beliefs, or pressured to take part in religious activities that are not of your choosing.

If you need certain days off from work, or if your faith requires you to wear a particular head covering, hairstyle, or facial hair, your employer must accommodate your sincerely held religious beliefs as long as doing so doesn't cause them undue hardship, such as:

★ Costing too much
★ Compromising workplace safety

GOOD FOR YOU!

Your employer must accommodate your sincerely held religious beliefs as long as doing so doesn't cause them undue hardship.

★ Decreasing workplace efficiency
★ Infringing on the rights of coworkers
★ Forcing coworkers to take on an unfair portion of your work

Religion and Anti-Discrimination Laws

Privately owned businesses and facilities that are open to the general public are known as public accommodations. The Civil Rights Act of 1964 prohibits public accommodations from discriminating against anyone based on their race, color, religion, sex, or national origin. Currently, there is no federal law prohibiting public accommodation discrimination based on sexual orientation or gender identification, but many states and local municipalities do have such laws.

Recent cases in Oregon and Colorado of bakers refusing on religious grounds to make wedding cakes for same-sex couples (and, in the Colorado case, also refusing to make a cake celebrating a customer's gender transition) have focused on whether the constitutional right to free exercise of religion trumps laws against discrimination in public accommodations. Similar cases have also come up of florists and wedding photographers refusing to provide services for same-sex weddings based on their religious beliefs.

Court rulings on these cases have varied on specific points, but overall the consensus is that where state or local laws prohibit discrimination in public accommodations, those providing such accommodations must follow the law.

Starting Your Own Church

In the United States churches are considered to be 501(c)(3) charities, which are exempt from paying federal, state, and local taxes. That means no property taxes on church-owned property, and (with certain exceptions) no income taxes on church revenue. The First Amendment's Free Practice Clause allows you to define your religion as whatever you want it to be. So can you enjoy freedom from taxes by starting your own church? Possibly.

Churches Versus Religious Organizations

The IRS distinguishes between churches (used as a generic term for all places of worship, including mosques and synagogues) and religious organizations, which it defines as "nondenominational ministries, interdenominational and ecumenical organizations, and other entities whose principal purpose is the study or advancement of religion."

Churches are automatically tax exempt, but religious organizations must apply to the IRS for tax-exempt status. In either case, tax-exempt status may be revoked if your church or religious organization engages in political or illegal activity.

Your church cannot be obviously run for your own personal benefit. It must provide some benefit to the community, whether through charitable activity or by holding religious services. You may, however, receive reasonable compensation as your church's minister.

Ministers Still Pay Income Tax

To become a minister and officiate at weddings, funerals, and other services, you can go to seminary school or become ordained for free through Get Ordained (getordained.org). Your pay as a minister is still subject to income taxes, but a reasonable amount of your pay may be designated as a tax-exempt housing allowance.

Resources for Religious Freedom

Blue Laws by State

worldpopulationreview.com/state-rankings/blue-laws-by-state

Find out which blue laws apply in the state you live in, or in a state you plan to visit.

A Parent's Guide to Religion in Public Schools

religiousfreedomcenter.org/wp-content/uploads/2015/01/
Parents-Guide-to-Religion-in-the-Public-Schools.pdf

Get answers to common questions about religion in public schools in this publication produced jointly by the National PTA and the First Amendment Center.

US Equal Employment Opportunity Commission (EEOC)–Religious Discrimination

eeoc.gov/religious-discrimination

The EEOC sets the bottom line on what constitutes religious discrimination in the workplace.

IRS Tax Guide for Churches & Religious Organizations

irs.gov/pub/irs-pdf/p1828.pdf

Here's everything you need to know to keep the IRS from knocking on the door of your new church.

Express Your Beliefs and Avoid the Bans

Social media jail is a walk in the park compared to actual jail. But if you're an avid user, being banned from a social media network can cut you off from vital personal and business connections and disrupt your normal life. Here's how to minimize your risk.

Big tech companies are in it for the money, and they'll do what they have to in order to protect their own interests—including maintaining a certain reputation. This could involve suspending or banning individual posts or entire accounts that they find troublesome or that are reported to violate their community standards (and found to, upon review). You do have some rights, but when it comes to "free" technology (remember: if you're not paying for the product, *you're the product*), your power is limited.

What Gets You Banned from Social Media?

Each social media platform has different standards for acceptable behavior and content. Here's a look at the standards across four of the biggies.

Facebook

According to Facebook's Community Standards page, you can be banned temporarily or permanently for:

★ Violent content or content promoting violence
★ Photos or videos of dangerous people or organizations
★ Content that encourages harm or crime
★ Posting goods and services that aren't allowed to be marketed through Facebook (including firearms)
★ Deceptive information
★ Content promoting suicide or self-harm, abuse, exploitation, or bullying
★ Words, images, or videos that violate someone's privacy
★ Objectionable content, including hate speech, graphic content, nudity, or sexual solicitation
★ Fake accounts or accounts used to spread spam or misinformation

Instagram

Most of the behaviors that'll get you banned from Facebook will also get you banned from Instagram, which should come as no surprise as they are both owned by Facebook's parent company, Meta.

Twitter

Twitter is not quick to ban users. In most cases, they'll take a less stern approach and flag or hide individual tweets instead of jailing an account. Here's what it'll take to get you banned from Twitter (temporarily or permanently):

★ Repeatedly spamming
★ Engaging in behaviors that put your account security at risk

- ★ A series or history of abusive or threatening tweets or direct messages
- ★ Promoting crime, including terrorism, child sexual exploitation, violent attacks, and hate crimes. Perpetrators of these crimes may also be banned from Twitter, regardless of whether or not they've posted about their illegal activities.
- ★ Sharing someone's private information
- ★ Impersonating someone else

TikTok

Like Twitter, TikTok takes a stepwise approach to content moderation. In most cases, your content will just be paused for review and removed if necessary. If your content goes against their policies, TikTok will send you a note detailing why it's been removed. This note is considered a first warning. Multiple warnings may lead to a temporary or permanent ban. Additionally, TikTok has a zero-tolerance policy for users who post certain things, such as:

- ★ Child sexual abuse material
- ★ Threatening public safety
- ★ Promoting self-harm
- ★ Sharing graphic or gory content
- ★ Promoting illegal activities
- ★ Threatening blackmail
- ★ Pretending to be someone else

How Do Social Media Platforms Handle Violations?

Facebook and Instagram

In some cases, Facebook and Instagram will mask content, so users must click on a post before seeing it. If that's not an appropriate response to the offending content, Facebook will initiate a temporary ban that lasts from a few hours to three weeks—or even permanently.

Twitter

Twitter handles things differently. It's unlikely you'll get a full-on account ban for one or two questionable tweets. Twitter's enforcement starts at the tweet level.

★ If your post contains disputed or false information, Twitter will affix a warning to that particular tweet.

★ If it's something particularly offensive or harmful, Twitter may require you to remove that tweet before posting anything new. In the meantime, they'll replace the tweet with a note about it violating their rules, so no one will be able to see it whether you remove it or not.

★ Rarely, Twitter may find a tweet questionable but feel they can't justify removing or hiding it because it's of public interest. In that case, they'll turn off engagements so others can't like, reply, or retweet.

At the direct message level, Twitter can block conversations between two users.

Twitter will only ban users who intentionally violate rules, ignore warnings, repeatedly violate policies, or post exceptionally harmful content. Before that, they'll usually try temporarily switching the account to read-only mode.

TikTok

TikTok only bans users for serious offenses. If your post seems off, TikTok will pause its publishing (or temporarily remove it if it's already been published) until their safety team can review it. If they decide to remove the video, they'll send a message letting you know why.

If you continue to post questionable videos, resulting in a second warning, TikTok will suspend your account temporarily. However, if that happens, you may still be able to access the platform as a view-only user. A temporary ban typically lasts a few hours to a week.

If you've received multiple warnings or posted something listed under their zero-tolerance policy, TikTok may permanently close your account.

The Problem with Social Media Jail

All the major social media networks will ban users for violent, harassing, or harmful content. Fair enough. Every person should have the right to exist in the social media universe without being threatened or harmed. Should posts promoting hate crimes or glorifying child abuse be filtered? Most would say yes. But the problem with social media jail lies in the subjective nature of censorship.

Who Decides What Gets Labeled as "Misinformation"?

It's very likely that the person reviewing your content on behalf of a social media platform is not an expert in the subject of your post. So how does the reviewer decide what's classified as misinformation? Is something considered misinformation if it doesn't align with how most people think? Unfortunately, if what you're sharing goes against what the masses believe to be accurate, it may also go against a social media platform's misinformation policy.

The Social Media Monopoly

We all know the big social media sharing platforms: Facebook, Instagram, Twitter, and TikTok. (They are considered different from social communication platforms, such as WhatsApp and Snapchat.) Some others have significant reach, but there's no doubt that the top four dominate the social media universe. For example, you probably have friends or acquaintances you only connect with through Facebook. When one of the major social media platforms bans you or censors your content, that can drastically affect your reach.

DID YOU KNOW?

Much of the social media review process is automated, which can lead to false flags.

Parts of the Review Process Are Automated

Social media companies cannot employ enough people to review every piece of content. Much of the process is automated. Many users report ending up in social media jail for liking too many of their friends' photos in a short period or sharing photos or videos falsely flagged as harmful.

Staying Out of Social Media Jail

The review system isn't perfect. You could do everything "right" and still find yourself banned from social media. To improve your chances of staying in Zuckerberg's good books:

★ Steer clear of conflict. If someone is less than great on social media, but their behavior doesn't affect you directly, choose to move on. The exception, of course, is if you see someone endangering or harming themself or others. In those instances, it's best to report their post, just in case.

★ Don't share contests and promotions unless you're sure the source is legitimate.

★ Recognize what's relevant (and allowed) on each platform.

★ Post higher quality content more often. Don't share every post that resonates with you. Posting too much in a short period can send signals to the social media bots that you're spamming.

★ Don't buy followers. Paying people to follow you isn't permitted on any of the major platforms.

★ Don't send friend or follow requests to strangers. You may get banned if they report that they don't know you.

★ Sign up with your real name and birth date. If you're reported for impersonating someone else, you'll need to prove your identity before regaining access to your account.

★ Don't copy and paste. If you post the same content on several groups or pages, you'll likely find yourself in temporary social media jail.

★ Keep it PG. If sharing racy content is your thing, that's cool. But make sure you find the proper outlet. The major social media platforms won't allow sexually suggestive content. If you're partial to "colorful" language, limit that to your "friends only" areas. Keep your language clean in groups and any space with an unrestricted audience.

What to Do If You've Been Jailed

You have the right to appeal the decision if you think you've been banned in error. That said, the review process can take quite a while, so if you've been banned temporarily, consider waiting it out.

If you've been banned permanently, then your alleged indiscretion must have been quite significant. You still have the right to appeal, but it's unlikely you'll get a reversal. If there's been a misunderstanding, be prepared to submit an explanation and supporting documents, such as an ID card confirming your identity.

You may be able to create a new account, but some social media networks will make it impossible to create a new account from your device or IP address. If that's the case, and you're desperate to get back on social media, you'll need to find a workaround.

Help or Hoax?
The First Amendment for Social Media

The First Amendment is often described as the amendment that protects our rights to freedom of expression. However, that description is somewhat oversimplified. The First Amendment prevents the government from passing laws limiting freedom of expression, religion, or peaceful assembly. Social media platforms are owned by private companies that can govern them as they please (within reason and as long as they aren't breaking any laws). **Because they aren't government-owned, the First Amendment doesn't apply to social media sites.**

Block Unwanted or Dangerous Contacts

Junk mail has been a scourge for generations, but nowadays it's joined by spam email, phone calls, and texts. Shut down that scammy "offer" for an extended car warranty and find more freedom in your day!

As long as you choose to be connected to the world around you, you will face unwanted intrusions by others with self-serving agendas—including spammers. You can't put an end to their efforts, but you can take action to protect your privacy and avoid getting scammed.

Email Spam

Email spam is big business. It's been estimated that a spammer will only get one response for every 12.5 million messages they send out, but because sending email costs essentially nothing, that tiny response rate can still earn millions of dollars per year.

Spam emails come in many flavors, but there are four basic kinds:

★ **Marketing for legitimate businesses.** Sometimes you sign up for these unintentionally, because you ordered something online and the consent for marketing email was buried in the fine print.

★ **Marketing for shady or fraudulent businesses.** These may offer unapproved medications, for example, or promise easy access to meds that need a prescription.

★ **Phishing.** These are clones of companies you know and already do business with. They aim to trick you into revealing your log-in and password or other sensitive information.

★ **Malware.** These entice you to open an attachment or click a link that will download malware onto your computer.

One Little Step for Protection

You may get perfectly legitimate emails from companies you do business with, such as your bank, a package delivery service, or your favorite online retailer. Often those emails will contain links for your convenience. However, because hackers and scammers can easily clone those emails, your safest practice is to avoid clicking any links, even if you trust the sender. Instead, take the time to leave your email program altogether, go directly to the purported sender's website, and see whether the information in the email is correct. If the email then seems suspicious to you, be sure to report it to the appropriate business.

GOOD FOR YOU!

Your safest email practice is to avoid clicking any links, even if you trust the sender.

Spam Filters

You're probably well aware of your email program's spam filter—perhaps you look in your spam folder now and then to make sure you're not missing a legitimate message, especially when email you're expecting doesn't seem to have arrived.

In the constant battle to keep your inbox spam-free, filters scan your incoming messages for:

★ **Suspicious IP addresses.** An internet protocol, or IP, address shows where out on the internet an email sender is located. If the IP address of an incoming message matches one associated with known spammers, a spam filter will divert it into the spam folder.

★ **Suspicious domains.** The sender's domain is the part of their email address after the @ sign. As with IP addresses, spam filters keep track of domains that have been used by spammers before.

★ **Spammy content.** Spammers are constantly upping their game, of course, but spam filters use machine learning to amass knowledge of the kind of language spammers use and block messages that fit those patterns.

★ **Spam reports.** Sometimes a spammer is able to format a spam message in a way that evades filters. If enough people notice and report that message, or similar messages from the same sender, eventually they'll end up on the blacklist.

Email Tracking

With email tracking, just opening an email may provide the sender with more of your personal information than you intended. Email tracking involves embedding a tiny bit of code—often, a single, invisible 1 x 1 pixel—that downloads when you click on a message and transmits data back to the sender. This can be as little as the fact you opened the message or as much as where, when, and on what device you opened it.

DID YOU KNOW?

Just opening an email may provide the sender with more of your personal information than you intended.

You can't stop others from using email trackers, but you can fight back. There are a number of email extensions, such as Ugly Email (uglyemail.com) you can download that will go through your inbox, tag any message that contains a tracker, and block the tracker.

The simplest and most commonly recommended action, though, is to stop your email program from automatically loading images (see Resources, at the end of the chapter, for instructions). This works because most email trackers come in the form of those little single pixels embedded in images, and if the images aren't loaded, the pixels aren't activated. Doing this won't catch every possible email tracker, but it's a good first step.

Email Account Hacking

With access to your email account, a spammer can bypass filters by using your trusted address to spam people in your contact list. If you are active online, your email address is likely stored in many more databases than you realize, and all of those databases are potentially vulnerable to hacking. To protect yourself (and your contacts) from hackers:

★ **Find out whether your email account has been hacked.** Use the website Have I Been Pwned (haveibeenpwned.com) to see whether your email address has been part of a data breach.

★ **Change your password.** Your email address is most valuable to a hacker, and most dangerous for you, when it's paired with your log-in password. If your email has been part of a data breach, you should change your password immediately. Experts disagree on whether or not changing your password at regular intervals, such as every ninety days, is really necessary if you use a strong one.

- ★ **Use a unique password.** Don't use the same password for your email that you use for other accounts.
- ★ **Use a password manager.** A password manager, such as 1password (1password.com), will both generate strong, unique passwords for every account you have and store them so all you need to remember is a single log-in.

Spam Phone Calls

If you screen your calls, only answering the ones you know are coming from someone you want to talk to, you're already taking the most effective step in protecting yourself from spam phone calls—not answering. As spammers and scammers get more sophisticated, though, even that may not be enough. Using voice over internet (VoIP) calling, they can easily spoof, or emulate, any number they choose, making you believe you're getting a call from a trusted contact.

Say Nothing

If you find you have accidentally answered a spam call, say nothing and press no buttons—just hang up and block the number. Most spam calls are robocalls that are autodialed by a computer. In some cases, they just want to see whether anyone answers, so they know they have a good number that can either be followed up with a call from a human or added to a list to be sold to scammers.

Any reaction or interaction on your part increases the chances that you will receive more calls in the future. There are even reports now of calls that start with you being asked,

DID YOU KNOW?

If you accidentally answer a spam call, say nothing and press no buttons—just hang up and block the number.

"Can you hear me?" only to have your "Yes" recorded and used to authorize fraudulent purchases or charges.

How to Stop Spam Calls

Use Your Phone's Blocking Features

You can (and should) block any individual number that you know or suspect is spam, but you should also be able to block incoming calls from any number not in your contact list. Depending on your phone, you may be able to activate "do not disturb" settings for certain times of the day or permanently block unknown callers. The downside to this is that you may sometimes get important calls from numbers not in your contact list, and you won't know unless they leave a voicemail.

Use Your Provider's Filtering and Blocking Features

Verizon, T-Mobile, and AT&T all have their own proprietary software to help identify incoming spam calls. Many other providers have their own programs, too, so check with yours to see what they offer. Services vary, may incur additional charges, and may not be available to all customers.

Use a Third-Party App

There are numerous apps you can download to help filter spam calls. They usually draw on lists of known spam numbers and also let you report new numbers that make it through the filter.

Add Your Number to the Do Not Call Registry

Scammers who know they are breaking laws aren't going to respect the DNC registry, especially if they are calling from outside the United States. Registering your number, though, may help drastically cut down on the number of spam calls you get.

The registry is operated by the Federal Trade Commission. Registering your number puts it on a list provided to telemarketers, who must remove all DNC numbers from their call lists within thirty-one days of registration. If you register and then get a call from a telemarketer after thirty-one days you can report them to the FTC, which has the power to impose penalties of up to $43,792 per call.

Companies you've done business with can still call you until you tell them to stop. Some other kinds of calls are exempt and can call, as long as they don't try to sell you anything, including:

* ★ Charities
* ★ Political organizations
* ★ Survey takers
* ★ Debt collectors

Spam Texts

As text messaging has become increasingly ubiquitous, it was inevitable spam texts would follow. These texts are generated by computers rather than by phones, and they can be sent out in large numbers at minimal expense, just as spam emails are. As with email spam, it only takes an occasional response to make the effort worthwhile.

★ As with other kinds of spam, your first defense is to **ignore messages from unknown senders**. Spammers will sometimes try to get around this commonsense defense, though, by pretending to be someone you trust, even someone in your contact list.

★ Just as with email, **never click on links in text messages**, even if they seem to come from someone you trust. Always go directly to the business website or otherwise independently verify the information in the text.

★ If you receive what seems like a perfectly legitimate text that is obviously meant for someone else, **delete it and block the number**. Sometimes the text will sound important—a business meeting that's been rescheduled, or a follow-up to a meeting that has already taken place—but don't get drawn in. If it's a genuine mistake, they'll figure it out without your help, and more likely it's just a clever way to get you to engage with the scammer when you would otherwise know better.

Unwanted Junk Mail

By now you are probably savvy enough not to conduct important business by snail mail, but may still be annoyed by quantities of junk mail arriving in your mailbox every day. You'll probably never be able to eliminate all of it, but there are measures you can take to reduce it.

Opt Out of Credit Card Prescreening

Go to OptOutPrescreen.com, the official, government-sanctioned site that lets you stop credit card companies from prescreening you and mailing you credit card offers. In addition to the annoyance factor, anyone who gets into your mailbox can help themselves to this kind of solicitation and may be able to open credit in your name.

GOOD FOR YOU!

Stop credit card companies from prescreening you and mailing you credit card offers.

Stop "Prospect" Mail

In the direct mail business, mail from companies you've never done business with is called "prospect" mail—you are a prospective customer they hope to entice. This is distinct from "customer/donor" mail, which comes from companies or charities you have patronized in the past.

Unlike spam emails or texts, printing and mailing prospect mail has real costs. While on the one hand a company may want to cast their net as widely as possible, it isn't worth it to send out materials that are going to go directly into the trash, so a marketing trade association has set up a service called DMAchoice that lets you opt out of prospect mail.

Signing up with DMAchoice (see Resources, below) will dramatically decrease the amount of prospect mail you get, but it won't keep you from getting customer/donor mail. For that you'll need to contact each business or charity directly and ask them to stop sending you unwanted mail.

Resources to Cut Off Unwanted Contacts

Stop Emails from Being Tracked

theverge.com/22288190/email-pixel-trackers-how-to-stop-images-automatic-download

Get illustrated instructions on turning off image loading.

Have I Been Pwned

haveibeenpwned.com

Find out in seconds if your email address has been part of a known data breach.

National Do Not Call Registry

donotcall.gov

Register your number, verify your registration status, and report unwanted calls.

OptOutPrescreen

optoutprescreen.com

Register on this site to opt out of credit prescreening and stop credit card solicitations from showing up in your mailbox.

DMAchoice

dmachoice.org

Use this site to opt out of junk mail from companies you haven't done business with.

Stay Out of Focus

Hundreds of thousands of security cameras are peppered throughout public spaces in the United States—they're in transit stations, schools, parks, stores, and even on public streets. But there are simple ways to avoid triggering any on-screen attention.

Avoiding surveillance cameras entirely is nearly impossible, and you're right to be concerned. Every time you leave your home you will inevitably be caught on surveillance cameras somewhere along the way, and it's impossible to predict how data collected in a public space will be processed, monitored, used, and stored.

So, do government and law enforcement agencies have the right to observe and monitor the behaviors of typical, law-abiding citizens? Legally, the answer is "yes"—they absolutely do have that right. You have some rights as well, but they may be more limited than you think.

Where Are Surveillance Cameras Found?

Legally, you have no expectation of privacy in public places, and surveillance cameras are common just about everywhere. How they record you, how long recordings are kept, and who can access them varies.

Stores and Restaurants

Most stores and restaurants are equipped with security systems that incorporate cameras. If you're shopping in a public retail space or eating at a food establishment, you should assume your actions are being monitored and recorded. Cameras in these environments are typically only accessible to the store owner and designated employees and are only shared with law enforcement if a crime, such as theft, occurs.

The footage is stored on a DVR (digital video recorder) or NVR (network video recorder). A DVR is not connected to the internet and has a limited storage capacity, so the video is overwritten within a month or two. An NVR may or may not be connected to the internet. If it's connected to the internet, an NVR system may use cloud storage, which is less secure than the physical storage of a DVR.

Parks

You'll find surveillance cameras in both city and state parks. They're intended to prevent crimes that typically occur in sparsely populated spaces late at night, such as drug dealing and graffiti, but they surveil the area 24/7. So while those cameras may catch the teenager who tagged the bench by the lake, they'll also see you walking your dog before work. Cameras in parks commonly run on an NVR system, and the footage is accessible to some government employees, such as park maintenance workers, as well as law enforcement.

Public Streets

Surveillance cameras may be placed on any public street, on buildings, in traffic lights, on toll booths, and more. Cameras placed by the government are used to monitor the behaviors of pedestrians and drivers alike. Footage from these NVR-connected cameras is monitored by government security employees and police.

Some government-placed cameras can capture detailed images, including license plate numbers. Individuals and businesses are also permitted to install cameras outside their properties. Unfortunately, there's no way to know who has access to these cameras, and some types, particularly those that rely on Wi-Fi, may be susceptible to security breaches.

Schools

More than 80 percent of public schools in the United States report using surveillance cameras as part of their security network. These cameras can be placed in lunchrooms, classrooms, hallways, auditoriums, and play areas. On the one hand, the cameras boost teacher accountability, but you might not be comfortable having your child recorded as they go about their school day.

Furthermore, when it comes to combating bullying, it seems that cameras are just pushing bullies and victims to more private spaces, such as bathrooms, where cameras are not allowed. This may actually increase the severity of the bullying.

Workplaces

It's illegal to capture audio in any space where employees may engage in a private conversation. Still, video-only cameras are likely scattered throughout your workplace, in all locations except for bathrooms and changing rooms. There's a place for cameras in a public-facing workspace but, unfortunately, there are no laws preventing employers from using surveillance cameras to

DID YOU KNOW?

More than 80 percent of public schools in the United States report using surveillance cameras.

monitor your computer usage or track the frequency and duration of your breaks.

Issues with Surveillance Cameras in Public Places

Recording Isn't Selective

A security camera that only records criminals would almost certainly be widely embraced by, well, anyone who isn't a criminal. However, tech companies have yet to perfect such a technology, and current surveillance cameras are not selective. So whether you're a violent criminal or a law-abiding citizen, a surveillance camera will monitor you in precisely the same way.

Consent Isn't Required

Surveillance cameras can't legally be set up in such a way as to record the inside of your house or apartment through a window, and they can't be installed in places such as bathrooms and changing rooms, where you expect to be alone. Aside from that, your consent isn't required to observe, record, or store video of you. Many people see this as a threat to consent and a step toward a dangerous future where consent is required less and less often.

Footage Can Be Misused

There's no (legal) limit to the number of people who can be granted access to security footage, as long as they work within an organization with legal access. There's no guarantee every store or government employee, tech support professional, or police officer with access to surveillance recordings will use them appropriately.

Effectiveness Is Unclear

There's mixed data on the effectiveness of surveillance cameras. For example, a person considering robbing a store may be deterred by that store's security system, but it's unlikely that the security system will prevent the crime entirely. In reality, it'll probably just encourage the criminal to commit the same crime elsewhere.

Some criminals, especially those committing more serious crimes such as mass shootings and suicide bombings, may be more likely to choose a location *with* surveillance cameras. They aren't hiding their actions; in some cases, they want to be recognized and publicized for their efforts.

Impossible to Guarantee Digital Security

Many security systems are monitored remotely, and footage is stored physically in a separate location or, worse, on a digital cloud-based platform. Any digital connection between where the video is recorded and where it's stored opens the door to hackers who may use the recording maliciously. Some of the world's largest and most secure agencies have fallen victim to hackers, and there's no way to guarantee security.

Protecting Your Privacy in Public Spaces

If you're in a public space, there's a good chance you'll encounter some type of surveillance. It's virtually impossible to avoid it entirely. That said, there are a few steps you can take to protect your privacy.

Blend In

The good news is that you'll rarely be the only person on a clip of security video footage. If you're wearing mainstream clothing and behaving typically, there's a slim chance you'll be targeted and monitored. While it may go against your core personal values, arguably the most effective way to maximize your privacy is to blend in with the crowd. The squeaky wheel gets the grease, so if you'd rather not be the center of attention in someone's security footage, don't be the squeaky wheel.

Keep Your Head Down

Facial recognition systems work much more effectively when they can snap a direct, front-facing photo. If you're out looking for security cameras, not only are you drawing attention to yourself by acting suspiciously, but when you find a camera, you're also giving it all the facial feature data it needs to identify you.

Shake Up Your Routine

Security cameras in public spaces can be used to track your habits. For example, if you take the same route every day and suddenly stray from that route, you may trigger an alert in a system that monitors patterns. If you routinely visit the same places, consider taking a different route or a different mode of transportation occasionally.

Resources for Understanding Surveillance

What's Wrong with Public Video Surveillance?

aclu.org/other/whats-wrong-public-video-surveillance

Read what the ACLU has to say about the dangers of surveillance cameras.

Video Surveillance of Public Places

cops.usdoj.gov/ric/Publications/cops-p097-pub.pdf

The US Department of Justice prepared this detailed guide for use by the police.

How to Thwart Facial Recognition and Other Surveillance

wired.com/story/how-to-thwart-facial-recognition-other-surveillance

You can take both low-tech and high-tech steps to protect your privacy in public places.

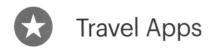 Travel Apps

Decide Whether Digital Routes Are Safe for You

You may need to choose between convenience and privacy risk when it comes to travel sites and apps. Here's what to consider the next time you want to get away.

Once upon a time, if you wanted to fly anywhere you had to pay a trained, licensed travel agent who could look up flights, make your reservation, and print your tickets. The travel agent could also arrange your hotel, ground transportation, and entertainment. Of course, if you had the time and know-how, you could always call hotels and make your own reservations, negotiate with cab drivers when you arrived in new cities, and stand in line for theater or theme park tickets—but since you were already paying the travel agent, you figured you might as well get your money's worth.

All that changed with the advent of the internet. In 1996, the online travel agency Travelocity pioneered self-serve, online travel booking, and the technology for DIY travel has exploded since then. Nowadays you can make virtually all your travel arrangements online in minutes, and keep everything handy with a suite of mobile apps on your phone.

As with so many other technological advancements, though, the convenience comes with a side of privacy risks: Studies by mobile security companies such as Pradeo and NowSecure have found that most travel apps are vulnerable to hacking and data breaches. There doesn't seem to be any way around providing the information these apps require, though—you can only decide whether the convenience is worth it.

Airline Apps

Most airlines now offer mobile apps that allow you to book flights and manage your bookings. With just your phone you can book flights, change your seats, order meals, check your frequent flyer miles, upload your COVID vaccination or testing status, and more. The app will alert you when it's time to check in, provide a digital boarding pass, let you know when your gate has been assigned, and notify you of any delays or changes.

The problem, of course, as with all technological conveniences, is that you must give up quite a lot of personal information in order to use these apps, and you have no control over how they manage or protect that information.

Testing by mobile security companies have found that the biggest risk with airline apps is that they transmit personal data over insecure networks, where it may be intercepted relatively easily. The apps have also been found to have weaknesses built in that make it possible for hackers to manipulate not just the information they contain but also the way they function. British Airways and Cathay Pacific, two major international airlines, have suffered hacks in recent years that exposed the personal data of thousands of customers.

Of course, you don't have to download or use the apps at all; you can still book and manage your flights by phone, as well as in person at the airport. However, the airlines will still store all your information; you just won't have access to it yourself. Before downloading an airline app, consider reading through the airline's privacy policy to see what information they collect on you.

A Warning for Boarding Passes

If you check in for your flight online, there's a good chance you'll have the opportunity to save a digital version of your boarding pass to your phone. If you worry about something going wrong, though, you may be inclined to print out a paper boarding pass anyway. And if you check a bag, the ticket agent is likely to print out a boarding pass and stick your luggage receipt to it.

Should you end up with a hard copy of your boarding pass by whatever means, leaving it behind on the plane, tossing it when you reach your destination, or posting a photo of it on social media isn't recommended. This is because barcode readers are readily available that allow anyone who picks up your boarding pass to scan its barcode and discover personal details such as your frequent flyer account number, phone number, passport number, and more.

To keep from inadvertently oversharing your personal information, keep your boarding pass safely tucked away until you can dispose of it securely.

GOOD FOR YOU!

Keep any printed boarding passes safely tucked away until you can dispose of them securely.

Online Travel Agencies

Online travel agencies (OTAs), such as Expedia and Priceline, offer a virtual version of the travel agent you used to visit in person. Besides pulling together travel deals from many different sources, OTAs may be able to offer you better rates than you might get if booking directly with an airline, hotel, car rental agency, or cruise line.

The trade-off is that when you book through an OTA you will have to provide the site with all relevant personal data, including credit card numbers and identification documentation (passport, driver's license, etc.). And because an OTA must communicate and share information with so many other websites and databases, booking through one provides multiple opportunities for your personal data to be accessed by bad actors. It's worth reading an aggregator's privacy policy to see how much of your personal information they collect, whether they share it with third parties, and how much control you have over your own data.

DID YOU KNOW?

Booking through just one online travel agency provides multiple opportunities for your personal data to be accessed by bad actors.

Travel Aggregators

Some sites, such as Skyscanner and Kayak, are basically travel search engines. After you enter your dates and destination, an aggregator will return results from airlines, hotels, car rental agencies, and OTAs, as appropriate, and provide links you can follow to make your bookings. You don't have to give up your personal information to an aggregator, and your privacy concerns are the same as when you use any other internet search engine—they primarily involve the use of cookies and selling of your search behavior to third parties.

Ride-Hailing Apps

Let's face it: Old-school travel is far more private. You can grab a taxi and pay cash for your ride, and your driver never has to know more than where they picked you up and where they dropped you off. As with all mobile travel apps, ride-hailing apps such as Lyft and Uber offer you convenience (and possibly a lower rate) in exchange for your personal information.

According to an analysis by Surfshark, a Netherlands-based VPN and cybersecurity company (see Resources, below), both Lyft and Uber—the most popular ride-hailing apps in the United States—"collect sensitive user information (sensitive information can include race, ethnicity, sexual orientation, pregnancy, childbirth information, religious, political, and philosophical beliefs, trade union membership, genetic information, or biometric data)." That's a lot more than is needed to get you from one place to another!

Smart Hotels

If you book hotel rooms through Booking.com or another online travel agency, or even online directly with a hotel, you face the same risks and concerns as with any other OTA. In addition, though, you may find yourself checking into a "smart" hotel that takes advantage of smart-home technology to make your stay more comfortable and more convenient.

In addition to basic functions such as checking in and opening your room door with the hotel's app, this technology may range from room service robots

Help or Hoax?

Digital Driver's License

Several states are trying out digital driver's license programs for those who already have physical licenses. After downloading the app, you either have your identity verified and the digital license activated in person or you set it up remotely by scanning the barcode on your license and taking a selfie that is consistent with your license photo.

You don't have to provide any information the licensing bureau doesn't already have, and there's no reason for them to track your activity. In fact, **this is the rare mobile app that actually enhances your privacy, at least during in-person interactions, as you decide how much information you want to share**.

For example, if you need to prove your age to make a purchase, you can ensure the other person sees only the bare minimum information required for the transaction. Even better, as digital licenses become more widely accepted, you will be increasingly able to use them contactlessly—you decide what information to share, your app creates a QR code that contains only that information, and the QR is scanned by the other party's device.

to devices that listen for your commands to dim the lights and turn up the heat.

The downsides to this convenience are not unexpected. For example, you may find the idea of a listening device in your hotel room a little unnerving, especially since Amazon admitted its Alexa speakers do record voices and employees do listen to them. Smart door keys use Bluetooth signals, which can be intercepted up to fifteen feet away. And if you are a frequent visitor to one hotel chain, they may track your movements and activities in order to customize your room preferences.

As with all mobile apps, you'll have to balance the perks of smart hotel technology with your desire to protect your privacy. You can always ask the hotel which smart features you can opt out of, see whether you can get a physical room key, and turn off or unplug devices in your room.

Theme Park Apps

Mobile security company Kryptowire (see Resources, below) lists the Disneyland app as the most invasive in terms of personal privacy, in large part because it accesses so many of your phone's features, such as its microphone, camera roll, Bluetooth, and location. It also tracks your activity within the park, including purchases you make and your usage of the app. Kryptowire gives Disney points for transparency in their privacy policy, but asks whether you really need an app to enjoy the theme park and suggests you delete it when you leave.

In addition to apps, many major theme parks, including Disney World, Universal Studios, and Six Flags, use fingerprint scanners to

match you up with your pass each time you enter. According to the parks, the scanners record and compare a few points of fingerprint geography—not enough to recreate the entire print. You may opt out of fingerprint scanning but will have to consent to having your photo taken instead, as the parks are invested in ensuring every person who enters has bought a legitimate pass.

Resources That Expose Travel App Risks

Apps with Excessive User Data Permissions

kryptowire.com/blog/popular-travel-ios-apps-request-excessive-user-data-permissions

You love your travel apps, but are you oversharing?

Airline Data Privacy Concerns

blog.pradeo.com/alarming-security-state-airline-mobile-apps

This summary report points out the most common travel app vulnerabilities.

A Look at Ride-Hailing and Taxi Apps

surfshark.com/blog/ride-hailing-taxi-apps-data-tracking

Find out how much of your personal data Lyft, Uber, and other ride-hailing apps collect.

Workplace Monitoring

Escape Employer Spying

While employers have many legitimate options for keeping tabs on their workers, legal lines can still be crossed. Know what privacy protections you can claim and how to see what your boss can see.

Employers have always kept a close eye on their employees. But with technological advances, employee monitoring in today's world expands far beyond the clock-in/clock-out process that we've been accepting since the 1800s, when the time clock entered mass production. With computers, tablets, smart phones and speakers, webcams, and all the other digital tools available today, all the world's knowledge is at your fingertips—and much of your personal information is now just as available to your boss.

How Can Your Employer Monitor You?

Phones

If your company-issued phone runs on Android (Samsung, Google, etc.) or iOS (Apple), they won't need to install any third-party software to track your device usage. Android and iOS both have that capability built in.

Mobile Device Management (MDM) Software

MDM software provides employers with remote access to a company-issued mobile device, such as a cell phone or tablet. It's inexpensive, quick to install, and easy to use. MDM software allows for activity monitoring (including screen mirroring) and location tracking. In addition, if an employee is terminated or loses a device, the software allows the employer to wipe the phone or tablet remotely.

Computers

If you're using a work-issued laptop or desktop computer, you'd better believe it's being monitored. With few exceptions, if a computer is connected to a network (wired or wireless), it's monitorable.

If you think you're in the clear because you've deleted your browsing history, think again. Cleaning out your browsing history does little to protect your privacy in the workplace. Some types of software provide employers with real-time access (screen mirroring), others offer periodic snapshots or whole-day video recordings, and some use key tracking and count mouse clicks.

Communications

Emails sent on a work computer are subject to monitoring, whether from a professional or personal email address. In addition, if you use other communication tools, such as Zoom, Slack, or Workspace, your employer can monitor those, too.

Your Personal Devices at Work

If your personal device is connected to your workplace's Wi-Fi, it's possible your employer can see what you're doing. Note, though, that it's illegal for your employer to monitor your personal devices

unless they've informed you verbally, in writing, or by way of company memos or onboarding documents.

Cameras

With a few exceptions, your employer can use cameras, overtly or otherwise, to track your activities in the workplace. (More on that below.)

Your Rights to Privacy as an Employee

Phone Conversations

Your employer has the right to listen in on any phone calls you make from a company phone, and they don't need to let you know they're listening. If they're actively listening and realize it's a personal call, they're supposed to disconnect, but realistically, who would know if they didn't?

American laws clearly differentiate between listening to a call and recording it. For recording, some states require two-party consent, where both people on the call must be aware it's being recorded. Other states require one-party consent. However, there's an exception for calls made from a business phone: Your employer can legally record any calls made or received with a company phone without consent, as long as the recordings aren't circulated outside the company.

Email Exchanges

Your employer can (and very likely does) read exchanges in your work inbox. If you choose to send a personal message from your work email address, your employer is entitled to read that message.

The laws surrounding your right to privacy when you access your personal email on a company device are unclear. Unfortunately, no law addresses that particular scenario, but courts usually side with the employer, stating that you forgo your right to privacy by using a device owned by someone else.

Browsing Habits

This one requires little explanation—the answer is "yes." Your employer has the right to see what websites you're visiting on a company device.

Cameras

Your employer isn't legally allowed to capture audio in spaces where employees may engage in private conversations, and they're not allowed to capture audio or video in bathrooms or changing areas. Aside from that, there are no laws protecting you from video surveillance in the workplace.

How to Tell Whether Your Employer Is Watching

Check Your Work-Issued Phone for Signs of Monitoring

If your work phone is iOS-powered, go to Settings > General > About. If your phone is being monitored using Apple's built-in tracking software, you'll see a message about the phone being supervised.

Your employer can manage your device through G Suite if you have an Android phone. Unfortunately, there's no way to confirm it from the device. Likewise, if your employer uses third-party tracking software, you may have difficulty finding out. Typically, a phone that's being tracked will have subpar battery performance. Beyond that, keep an eye out for the GPS tracking symbol at the top of the screen. Someone might be tracking you if you see it pop up and you're not using an app that needs your physical location.

Check for Background Processes on Your Computer

Some advanced programs run in "stealth" mode and won't appear in your system's list of running programs. Unfortunately, those are virtually impossible to detect unless you're a tech pro. However, many monitoring programs will show up in your device's Task Manager (PC) or Activity Monitor (Mac).

If you're using a PC with Windows, press CTRL, ALT, and DEL all at once, then click Task Manager to see which processes are active on the computer. If there's a program you don't recognize, search its name on the web to find out what it does.

If you're using a Mac, open Utilities and navigate to the Activity Monitor section. Again, if there's a name you don't recognize, run a web search to figure out the program's purpose.

Look for Hidden Cameras in Your Workspace

You can buy a decent hidden camera detector for under $100, but there are other ways to detect hidden cameras.

First, if a camera has a night vision feature, you should be able to see a red glow when night vision is active. Turn off all the lights and check common hiding places, including smoke detectors, shelves, plants, under furniture, and on or around light fixtures and wall decor.

If you don't see any signs of a night vision camera, shine a flashlight around the room. A camera's lens would reflect light toward you, so if you shine your flashlight on a dull object and there's a small shiny spot, that could be a hidden camera.

Finally, call someone you can trust (ideally, someone who's in on your plan) and keep them on the phone while you walk around the room. Some cameras produce interference, and you may hear a slight static noise when you're near one.

Protecting Your Privacy in the Workplace

If your employer pays the bill for the phone you're using, whether it's a landline or a company smartphone, you should assume it's being monitored. Otherwise, to protect your privacy:

★ Limit private conversations to private spaces. If you'd like to discuss something sensitive with a colleague, ask them to meet up outside work. If that's not practical, ask to meet in the washroom. (As long as it's a multi-stall washroom and not a single, one-person-at-a-time restroom, of course.)

★ If you're doing something personal online, do it from a device you own and connect to your cell provider's data network instead of the company Wi-Fi.

★ Tack a sticky note over your computer's webcam if you're not comfortable with the idea of your employer watching you work.

A Note on Working from Home

With the onset of the COVID pandemic in 2020 came an uptick in the number of employees working remotely. While most workplaces have reopened for in-person work, some employers have given employees the option of working from home permanently. This shift has caused issues for employers who monitor their employees exceptionally closely, and they've found ways around it.

Your employer may ask you to install an activity tracker while you're on the clock, and legally, they have every right to require it. They'll also still have access to your company email and other workplace communication channels, regardless of whether you're using a personal device. If you find intrusions of this kind unacceptable, your only real recourse is to refuse and, likely, find another job.

Resources for Workplace Privacy

Surveillance at Work

workplacefairness.org/workplace-surveillance

Get answers to questions about how your boss can monitor you.

Protection from Workplace Overreach

epic.org/issues/data-protection/workplace-privacy

The Electronic Privacy Information Center (EPIC) has been reporting on and advocating for digital privacy since 1994.

"Bossware" Tracking

eff.org/deeplinks/2020/06/inside-invasive-secretive-bossware-tracking-workers

The Electronic Frontier Foundation (EFF) has been around even longer than EPIC, with similar goals.

Index

Twitter, 226–227, 228–229, 230. *See
also* social media

U

V

W